The Other Side of Courageous

Helping you on your journey
back to the Courageous Side of life

Lynn Wheeler

PRESS

TABLE OF CONTENTS

INTRODUCTION

I was sitting in a restaurant in Nashville, Tennessee, having a meal with my long-time friend, Terry Bailey. I always try to connect with Terry whenever I am passing through Nashville. He has been a true friend to me, and I always enjoy hanging out with him.

About halfway through the meal, Terry asked me a question that would radically change my life and birth an idea for a new book. He simply asked, "Lynn, have you seen the movie *Courageous* yet?" When I answered no, he rushed me through my meal, saying, "Hurry and eat. We are going to go see it right now!"

As I sat there and watched that movie, my heart pounded and tears flowed. It had an incredible impact on me, as it has on many others. I left committed to becoming a better husband and father. A few weeks later, I watched it with my family. After it was over, I went to the master bathroom in my house and cried again. My wife, Dianna, came in, and we cried together. It was a powerful and life-altering movie.

In my time of processing what this movie spoke to me, I began to really think about something. My thoughts provoked a question: what about those on the *other side* of courageous? By that I mean, what about those who want to make such a pledge but have been wounded and rejected and thus struggle to make such drastic change? What about those of us who have already blown it? What about those whose daily struggles are sometimes more than they can bear? I am one of those men.

On the other side of courageous are many broken people and families. These people have no idea how to get back to the courageous side. It is in their hearts to do so, but they cannot do it alone. The pain is too intense and the memories too powerful.

In this book, we will look at some things to help us get back to the courageous side. I will share personal experiences and scriptures that I pray will bring healing and hope to you. The Lord will help us deal with all the emotion and scars of past relational disasters. He will lead us back to *courageous*!

The bottom line is, I want to be better. Do you? Let's take a journey together through the *other side of courageous!*

FORWARD

We all like to talk about our successes and about how courageous we are as we journey through life. However, we rarely like to talk about "the other side of courageous." The place where we struggle, suffer, and even fail. Lynn's book will provide deep ministry to your heart and life as he shares about his own struggles and failures on the "other side of courageous." This book will not only give you deep insight into Lynn's own life, it will help you successfully navigate through the obstacles we all wrestle with on the "other side of courageous." This book will be a tremendous blessing to you during your journey through life's toughest battles!

Herbert Cooper
Lead Pastor
Peoples Church
Oklahoma City, Oklahoma

Wounded Warrior

I was sitting in a Panera Bread café in Mobile, Alabama, when the call came. I was having coffee with my friend and colleague, Glenn Badonsky. I was listening intently to his victory reports and hearing his vision for India and future ministry there. With one phone call, however, my emotions went from rejoicing with one friend to being heartbroken for another.

The call was from a friend that I will call "Bo" throughout this story. Bo rarely called me. Even though he was a pastor and I was an occasional ministry guest in his church, we did most of our communicating through texts and e-mails. When I saw his name on my phone, I immediately sensed something was wrong. I asked Glenn to excuse me and took the call.

In a shaky voice, Bo said, "Hey, Lynn, are you busy?" I had barely gotten the words out of my mouth that I could talk when Bo broke into tears. Crying uncontrollably, he announced to me that his wife was leaving him. My heart was pounding, and I quietly began to ask the Lord to give me the words to help my friend. Between his hysterical sobs, I tried to ask questions. My friend was broken and wounded. I felt helpless. Within a few minutes, Bo calmed enough to tell me the story.

You see, Bo's wife was leaving, but it was his fault. For the second time in his life, he had been involved in an inappropriate relationship with another woman. This time his wife was not so forgiving, and their marriage was in serious trouble. Bo was guilty, and it was going to cost him his family.

Yes, he was broken and wounded. However, it was all the result of his wrong choices and bad decisions. There was nowhere else to lay the blame; he alone was responsible. This wounded warrior was broken and emotionally falling apart, but all I could do was pray and stand by my friend, even in his mistake. Sadly, his marriage ended in divorce, and his life was forever altered.

Many of us can relate to Bo. We harbor emotional pain and wounds in our lives that were brought on by our own failures. Bad decisions, wrong choices, lack of discipline, and even sin have played a part. In my own life, I could have done many things differently in my first marriage. Because I didn't, the wounds can still be reopened at times. I could have done some things differently in being a dad; because I didn't, the wounds can still be reopened.

When a wound is reopened, it is as if you are reliving the situation all over again. Here are some things I would encourage you to do when you are trying to help a friend who has been wounded through his or her own fault:

1. Do not judge the person.

   "There is only one lawgiver and Judge; the one who is able to save and destroy. But you—who are you to judge your neighbor?" (James 1:12).

   "Do not judge, or you too will be judged. For in the same way you judge others, you will be judged, and with the measure you use, it will be measured to you" (Matt. 7:1–2).

   "For God will bring every deed into judgment, including every hidden thing, whether it is good or evil" (Eccles. 12:14).

   God will bring the deeds of our lives into judgment—not us!

2. Do not offer false hope.

   I could not tell Bo that he could just go on pastoring his church and everything would be fine. That would have been offering him false hope. Even though our friends may be in pain and wounded, if they brought it on themselves, they will eventually have to face the consequences. You can stand by them without condoning what they have done or offering false hope.

3. Do not betray the confidence.

Some people feel like they have to tell everything they know — even confidential information from their friends. *Do not* betray this confidence! You are dealing with a wounded person. I have been a wounded person, and I know this: we are very sensitive and fragile when the wound is still fresh. Even after it heals, it can easily be reopened. Take the high road and be a person who can be trusted with other people's failures.

As the Scriptures remind us, "Now it is required that those who have been given a trust must prove faithful" (1 Cor. 4:2).

If you are a person who relishes others' failures and feel like you have to talk about it and magnify it — *don't do it!* Let God change your heart now.

The Word of God gives an example of a wounded warrior. In fact, Jesus Himself tells the story. We know it as the parable of the good Samaritan, and it is found in Luke 10:30–37.

This parable was prompted by a question from an expert in the law: "Who is my neighbor?" (Luke 10:29). Jesus began by talking about a man traveling down a road from Jerusalem to Jericho. The road Jesus was referring to was very narrow in many places, making it easy for robbers to hide among the rocks. This seventeen-mile road featured a 3,300-foot descent.

Interestingly, the word *Jerusalem* means "place of glory," and *Jericho* means "broken place." So the Samaritan was on his way from a place of glory to a broken place, and in the process he became a broken person, a wounded warrior.

How do you respond to broken people? I have often used the example of a threatening waterfall to illustrate possible responses. This will require some imagination on your part, but here we go.

I need you to envision a flowing river. (Come on and play my game!) See it? Okay. Now you need to imagine a raft floating on that river. Got it? Good. Now you need to see me in that raft. See it? Awesome! Now look down that river and see a waterfall at the end. Picture me in the raft as it heads toward the waterfall.

There are five categories that describe how people might respond in such a scenario:

1. Some people might yell from the shore, "Hey, Lynn! You are headed toward a waterfall!" That's it? Yes, that is all they have. Thank you, Captain Obvious!
2. Others would yell from the shore, "Hey, Lynn! You are headed for a waterfall, but I am praying for you!" To those I would respond, "Thank you so much, but right now, I need more than prayer!"

3. Some would acknowledge the waterfall and then say, "Let's talk about it. When did you first get into the water? Meet me at Starbucks and we will discuss it." But the problem is, I need more than talk at this point!

4. Still others would say, "I'll go get somebody to help you." Well, chances are good that I do not have that much time.

5. The final response is from the person who will jump into the water, swim to my raft, and help me get safely to shore.

Now we all know people who fit into each one of those categories. My question is, where do you fit? Which category above best describes you?

Let's return to the parable of the good Samaritan and examine the characters in this well-known story. First of all, Jesus mentioned robbers. John 10:10 tells us that the devil comes to steal, kill, and destroy. What the robbers did to this man sure sounds like what the devil has done and wants to do to us. Let's take a look:

a. They stripped him—brought humiliation.
b. They beat him—inflicted pain.
c. They went away—deserted him.
d. They left him half-dead—but he was half-alive.

The enemy of your soul has come to humiliate you, inflict pain on you, and desert you. He will then leave you half-dead. The only good news is that you are still half-alive! Jesus has a reputation of restoring broken people and wounded warriors. As He says in Jeremiah 30:17, "But I will restore you to health and heal your wounds."

Second, let's look at the priest and the Levite in this story. They represent the religious crowd. Keep in mind, the Levites of the Old Testament were the singers. So here we have the preacher and the worship leader who saw the man in need but merely passed by on the other side of the road. What? Seriously? Not all preachers and worship leaders would respond that way, only those who have an emphasis on religion and rules rather than on relationship and grace.

Let's stop for a moment and look at what "religion" looks like:

1. It focuses more on rules than on relationships.
2. It wants people to conform to outward standards of methods, dress, etc. instead of being like Jesus.
3. It walks *around* broken people—not toward them—and sometimes even criticizes them. *Never criticize a wounded warrior!* You do not know the fullness of the story.

Religion will fail you when you are walking through a character assassination. It will fail you when you experience financial lack. It will fail you when you are under physical attack and your friends desert you. But whereas religion will sooner or later fail, a relationship with Jesus will not! He is your

17

sustainer through it all. As 2 Timothy 2:19 says, "God's solid foundation stands firm."

Third, let's look at the Samaritan and how his actions parallel the actions of Jesus:

a. He saw the man in need and took pity on him. In other words, he cared.

b. He took the initiative to approach the man. The man was so injured that somebody had to go to him.

c. He bandaged the man's wounds. Now it really got messy! Now he was going to get some blood on his hands. This was much more than merely saying, "I am praying for you."

d. He poured in the oil and the wine. The oil was intended to keep the wounds soft, and the wine was used to sterilize them.

e. He put the man on his own donkey, which meant the Samaritan now had to walk.

f. He took the man to an inn and secured a room for him with advance payment.

g. He went back to check on him—because he cared!

Friends, it costs a lot to restore the half-dead. It costs a lot of money, time, and energy. I realize some people are wounded because of their own actions. Wrong choices, bad decisions, and even sin have left them lying in a ditch somewhere. It does not matter how they got there; it matters that they are there. They are wounded, and that matters to God.

My brother, Dennis, is four years younger than I. When we were boys, we often watched army movies on TV and then went out to play army in the yard. We would separate ourselves by several yards and begin launching rocks (grenades) at each other. I would pull the imaginary cord, even make the appropriate noise, and then launch it in my brother's direction. When the make-believe grenade landed close enough to him, I would make a noise as if I had just blown him up.

One day when we were playing, I launched a rock (grenade) in his direction, throwing it high into the air. He looked up just in time to have that rock hit him in the face, right below his eye. Immediately I felt pain in my backside because I knew my parents were going to bust me one. I knew I had to run into the house ahead of my brother and make up the best lie I could, something that might keep me out of trouble. I hurried into the house and told my mom that my brother had thrown the rock into the air himself, and when he looked up, it came down and hit him in the face. (I have since asked for forgiveness!)

My mom did not care how it happened; she just knew that her son was badly injured. My parents hurriedly wrapped my brother's face in a towel, and we all loaded into the car and sped toward the hospital. My brother was screaming and my mom was crying as my dad tried to navigate traffic as quickly and safely as possible. Finally we arrived at the emergency room. We all jumped out of the car, and as we walked through the doors, doctors and nurses rushed to our aid. They took my brother into a room, and I stood at the door and watched. Even though I was only eight years old at the time, I remember the event like it was yesterday.

I stood there and watched as doctors cleaned the blood off my brother's face. My mom held down his legs as they stitched him up. During this process, my mom turned to me and asked, "Where is your father?" I had not even noticed that he had not followed us in. I had no idea where he was.

Then Mom said, "Go find your father. Hurry!" I walked out the door of the hospital and headed toward the car. When I glanced to the right, I saw my dad leaning against the wall of the hospital, crying.

I walked over and said, "Dad, Mom wants you." With tears flowing down his face, my dad said, "Son, I cannot go in there. I cannot stand to see my son suffering and crying."

If earthly fathers feel that way about their children, how much more does our heavenly Father feel that way about us? He has been touched with the feeling of our infirmities. He does not want to see His children suffer. It does not matter why they are wounded—they just are.

Truthfully, I will always remember those who walked "on the other side" when I was a wounded warrior lying in a ditch half-dead. You see, some of those people were my "friends." But the years have passed, and that has helped to soothe my anger, bitterness, and confusion. More importantly, I have learned that those kinds of things have to be left in the hands of the Lord; there is no other way to deal with them.

I also will never forget those who stopped and poured in the oil and wine, those who nursed me back to mental, spiritual, and emotional health. These were the ones who took time to help me. I am alive today because of them, and I will never forget them—*never!*

Questions for Discussion:

1. Why is it wrong to judge people who have fallen? Have you ever had people judge you? Discuss the feeling that caused in you.
2. Why is it never a good idea to offer false hope?
3. Has someone ever betrayed your confidence? Discuss the hurt and damage it caused.
4. Were you surprised by the people who walked around you when you were wounded and lying in the ditch?
5. Describe the value of those who stopped and helped your healing process.

GET ON YOUR KNEES
AND FIGHT LIKE A MAN

I graduated from Bible college in May of 1982. Immediately I began to travel the United States as an evangelist. Being a traveling minister then was completely different from the way it is now. Some of the changes are good, but some are not so good.

One of the things that has changed (thankfully) is the lodging for the guest speaker. Back in the early 1980s, traveling ministers generally stayed in designated evangelist quarters or at the pastor's house. Staying in the pastor's home usually meant that one of his kids got kicked out of their room for a week—not a good start in relationship building with a child! Additionally, the evangelist found himself suddenly living with people he did not know. In my own experience, I had many awkward and humorous moments staying in pastors' homes.

The evangelist quarters in the church was always scary! As my friend Alton Garrison says, "Demons play football in churches at night." Can you imagine how many creaks and other noises you hear when staying alone in a strange place? On more than one occasion, I was reduced from "God's man of faith and power" really fast. On other occasions, I had someone walk in on me. It definitely kept me on my toes—in every way. For those churches who still use evangelist quarters, please understand that I am not making fun of you. I'm just thankful they are no longer the norm. Hampton Inn, please!

In my early days of traveling, I often preached in a small Oklahoma town called Fairview. The pastor there was a wonderful man named James Mabry. He was a great blessing to me as a young minister. His kindness and guidance will never be forgotten.

The thing that stands out to me the most about Pastor Mabry is that he was *always* praying. He would spend time praying at the church, and then when he got home, he would pray some more. I would hear him praying in his room, calling out to God, and it left a deep impression on me as a young minister. It seemed to me that was all Pastor Mabry did—pray! When I asked his family about it, they confirmed that he always prayed like everything depended on God, which, of course, it does.

I am asking God to help all of us in this area. Remember, praying not only changes things, but it also changes people. Your prayer time enhances and strengthens your relationship with God. Your relationship with God affects your relationships with others. Likewise, your relationship with others affects your relationship with God. That is not the only reason we need to get on our knees and fight like a man, but it is an important one.

There is a certain prayer that gets my attention every time I read it in Scripture. It is a prayer from Jesus Himself. Let's look at Matthew 26:36–45,

Then Jesus went with his disciples to a place called Gethsemane, and he said to them, "Sit here while I go over there and pray." He took Peter and the two sons of Zebedee along with him, and he began to be sorrowful and troubled. Then he said to them, "My soul is overwhelmed with sorrow to the point of death. Stay here and keep watch with me."

Going a little further, he fell with his face to the ground and prayed, "My Father, if it is possible, may this cup be taken from me."

Then he returned to his disciples and found them sleeping. "Could you men not keep watch with me for one hour?" he asked Peter. "Watch and pray so that you will not fall in to temptation. The spirit is willing but the body is weak."

He went away a second time and prayed, "My Father, if it is not possible for this cup to be taken away unless I drink it, may your will be done."

When he came back, he again found them sleeping because their eyes were heavy. So he left them and went away once more and prayed the third time, saying the same thing.

Then he returned to the disciples and said to them, "Are you still sleeping and resting? Look, the hour is near, and the Son of Man is betrayed into the hands of sinners. Rise, let us go! Here comes my betrayer."

This is one of the most intense prayer times recorded in Scripture. In His hurt, heartache, and confusion, Jesus called out to God, His Father. In great distress, He encouraged His friends to pray with Him. In this moment, Jesus experienced something we have all faced as well. It bears the question, what do you do when heaven is silent and your best friends are asleep? We have all been there. What do you do when you cry out to God, but get no response, when you need people to pray with you, but no one is willing?

Prayer brings a much-needed power into our lives. Jesus told the disciples to go to Jerusalem and pray until they received *power* (Acts 1:8). A story that illustrates this point is the story of a man named John Hyde, also known as "praying John Hyde." This man was a great preacher because he was a great prayer warrior.

One night John Hyde was attending a meeting where another man was preaching the gospel. The minister noticed John in the audience, and after he read his text, he called him to the front to pray over the message. Because John was a man of prayer, he was also a man of power. He walked up to the microphone and said, "Jesus." Then he said it again: "Jesus." The third time he said the name of Jesus, people got up and began to run to the altar to accept the Lord into their hearts. That is the power of prayer!

Let's look at three things about prayer:

1. APPROACH TO PRAYER

a. Focus more on being with God than getting from God.

b. Create the right atmosphere. This helps you move from the physical realm of prayer time to the spiritual realm of being with God. Play worship music or retreat to a place of solitude. Do whatever works for you, but remember, atmosphere is important.

c. Realize that prayer is hard work. If it weren't, everyone would be doing it. As someone has said, "Prayer is not preparation for the battle; prayer is the battle." Sometimes when we come out of prayer, we are exhausted.

d. Understand that prayer provides an opportunity to improve your relationship with God with response from Him (2 Chron. 7:14).

2. GOOD HABITS OF PRAYER

It takes time to form a habit—twenty-one days, in fact. Stay with the habit of prayer until it becomes a normal part of your day.

a. Pray the Word. The Bible records more than eighty personal prayers.

b. Pray according to God's will.

c. Pray in the Spirit (Rom. 8:27; Jude 1:20).

d. Pray with understanding (1 Cor. 14:15).

e. Pray warfare prayers.

f. Pray with a journal close at hand. I have often found it helpful to write down things the Lord impresses on me during my prayer time.

3. ESSENTIALS OF PRAYER

a. Repentance (Ps. 24: 3–5; 1 John 1:9)

b. Forgiveness (Mark 11:25)

c. Obedience (1 Sam. 15:22; Heb. 5:7)

d. Persistence (Luke 18:1; Col. 4:2)—To devote yourself to prayer means to continue steadfastly, or to persevere.

e. Agreement (Matt. 18:19; Lev. 26:8)—I would encourage everyone to find an agreement partner (Eccles. 4:9–10).

f. Faith (Matt. 17:20; Mark 9:21–24)

g. Confidence—This will help you fall asleep in a lion's den and have no fear of a burning furnace.

h. Profession—A positive declaration of faith is something powerful and effective. Do it (Mark 11:22–26).

i. Specificity (Mark 10:51)

j. Spontaneity—Matthew, Mark, and Luke all record the story of the woman who anointed Jesus with perfume from her alabaster box. This was a spontaneous act apart from any arbitrary standard of godliness.

k. Expectation—Three times in 1 Kings 17, Elijah stretched himself out on a dead boy, expecting him to come back to life, which he did (v. 22).

l. Boldness—Boldness overcomes darkness (1 John 4:4).

m. Patience (Heb. 10:35–36)

Get on your knees and fight like a man—pray!

Questions for Discussion:

1. Do you have a consistent prayer life? Why or why not?
2. If prayer changes things and people, why doesn't everyone do it? What are the major hindrances to prayer?
3. Why is praying with a journal close at hand a good idea?
4. Think about your communication with God. Would you say you talk more or listen more? Talk about the value of both.
5. Are you capable of changing your prayer habits? Do you need an accountability partner to help you accomplish that?

FORGIVENESS
IS FOR GIVING

❧

*A*s a minister of the gospel, I have heard a lot of people's stories. Some were stories of great victories, while others were stories of dark despair. Some of the stories brought a smile to my face and joy to my heart, while others brought tears to my eyes and a lump in my throat. Some were easy to listen to, and the time flew by as I absorbed the story; while others were hard to bear and made me want to jump up and run away. Through the years, I have experienced a wide range of emotion from listening to people tell me their stories.

Most of the stories that made me want to run or put a lump in my throat were centered around people who had been wronged by others. Some were lied to, some were abandoned, some were emotionally damaged—the list goes on and on. In many cases, those who were telling me the stories spoke sharply, their words laced with bitterness. I could practically see the fire shooting from their eyes and could hear the harshness in their tone. Though these people struggled with many different problems, the root of all those problems could be summed up in one word— *unforgiveness*. They simply could not let go of the wrong that had been done to them. What a dangerous place to be!

When you refuse to forgive, you are hurting yourself more than the person you will not forgive. By forgiving someone who has hurt you, you release yourself to a new and higher level in your relationship with God. When there are broken or strained relationships in your life, forgiving becomes an issue to be dealt with.

One of my favorite Bible characters is Joseph. I love to read about him and teach from the Scriptures about his life. What a roller-coaster ride his life was! Look with me for a moment at a particular story about Joseph that truly amazes me.

We are going to visit Joseph's family at a very sensitive time. Seventeen years had passed since they were reunited. Genesis 47:28 tells us that Joseph's father, Jacob, was now 147 years old. In all these years, his family had survived quite a bit. They had survived both separation and a devastating famine, but eventually they were reunited.

In our story, Joseph received word that his father was very sick. Genesis 49:33 records the patriarch's death: "When Jacob had finished giving instructions to his sons, he drew his feet up into the bed, breathed his last breath and was gathered to his people."

Joseph spent the first seventeen years of his life and the last seventeen years of his life with his father.

Now, for the second time in his life, they were separated. His reaction is recorded in scripture: "Joseph threw himself upon his father and wept over him and kissed him. Then Joseph directed the physicians in his service to embalm his father Israel. So the physicians embalmed him, taking a full forty days, for that was the time required for embalming. And the Egyptians mourned for him for seventy days" (Gen. 50:1–3).

The loss of a family member brings quite a few emotions and reactions to the surface. The one subject that surfaced in Joseph's family after his father's death was forgiveness. Joseph's brothers immediately began to question whether Joseph had *really* forgiven them for selling him into slavery and lying to their father about what had happened to him. Let's examine the Scriptures and see what we discover.

1. Joseph's forgiveness was real: "When Joseph's brothers saw that their father was dead, they said, 'What if Joseph holds a grudge against us and pays us back for all the wrongs we did to him?' So they sent word to Joseph, saying, 'Your father left these instructions before he died: "This is what you are to say to Joseph: I ask you to forgive your brothers the sins and wrongs they committed in treating you so badly." Now please forgive the sins of the servants of the God of your father.' When their message came to him, Joseph wept" (Gen. 50:15–17.)

After seventeen years, Joseph's brothers were still not sure he had really forgiven them. Did Joseph just act it out while his father was alive? Joseph's reaction tells us his forgiveness was real: he wept.

It broke his heart that his brothers had not believed him. Now that their father was dead, their imagination began to run wild.

Imagination is a powerful thing. Most of the things we imagine are not real or will never happen. However, there are times when we all have a tendency to let our minds run wild with imagination.

I attended Central Bible College in Springfield, Missouri. It was about a four-and-a-half-hour drive from my hometown, Oklahoma City. As a college student, I made that trip many times.

One year I was coming home for Christmas break. A friend of mine, who was from Tulsa, was with me. Since I had to go right through Tulsa, I was going to drop her off at her house before I continued home. Since we both had to work that day, it was after dark before we were finally Oklahoma bound.

We were only about twenty miles outside of Springfield when I hit some black ice on I-44. My car went into a spin, and we ended up in a ditch. We were both scared, but physically all right. However, our McDonald's french fries were scattered everywhere. I hate losing even one of those!

A highway patrolman came by and picked us up. He kindly gave us a ride back to CBC, and the next day, my car was towed back as well. The next day, my dad drove from Oklahoma City and picked us up.

The reason I shared that story is that to this day, whenever I have to drive on ice, I remember that spin. My imagination takes over. I hate it, but it does. So now I hate driving on ice. Even if I am moving along fine, I can see myself in that spin on the interstate. The memory sometimes paralyzes me. You very spiritual people who have no issues to deal with, please pray for me! Imagination is a powerful thing. Joseph's brothers were imagining something that wasn't even there.

2. Joseph's forgiveness was permanent: "But Joseph said to them, 'Don't be afraid. Am I in the place of God? You intended to harm me, but God intended it for good to accomplish what is now being done, the saving of many lives. So then, don't be afraid, I will provide for you and your children.' And he reassured them and spoke kindly to them" (Gen. 50:19–21).

True forgiveness does not say "I forgive you" today and then take it back tomorrow. The Lord has not done that to us, and we cannot do that to others. Paul wrote, "Be kind and compassionate to one another, forgiving each other, just as in Christ, God forgave you" (Eph. 4:32).

Joseph put action behind his words. "I will provide for you and your little ones," he said. Wow, what a defining moment! For someone to tell me they will take care of me is one thing, but when they say they will be good to my kids, that is even better!

Be sure to guard your heart, even when you have the power to place guilt on someone else. Refuse to rub their nose in the mess they have made. Extend grace and forgiveness that is eternal, not temporary, just like Joseph did.

I once heard a story about a man who was dying of rabies. The doctors had tried for months to save him but could not. They finally gave the man the news that they had done all they could do and he was going to die. The doctors continued to come by to visit him and keep him as comfortable as possible.

One day a doctor came by and noticed that the man was writing intently. The doctor asked if he was writing out instructions for his family. The man replied, "No, I am making a list of all the people I am going to bite before I die!" I'm sure that is just a joke, but it is a great example of a man who has not exercised the power of forgiveness in his life.

3. Joseph's forgiveness set him free: "Then Joseph said to his brothers, 'I am about to die. But God will surely come to your aid and take you up out of this land to the land he promised on oath to Abraham, Isaac and Jacob.' . . . So Joseph died at the age of a hundred and ten. And after they embalmed him, he was placed in a coffin in Egypt" (Gen. 50:24, 26).

What an illustration of the power of forgiveness! It released Joseph to die at peace with himself and those around him. His integrity, faith, and ability to forgive those who had wronged him make him a spiritual giant in my book.

Whom do you need to forgive today? What is it that you need to let go of? Colossians 3:13 says, "Bear with each other and forgive whatever grievances you may have against one another. Forgive as the Lord forgave you."

I served as youth pastor at Crossroads Church in Oklahoma City, Oklahoma, from 1985 to 1989. It was a privilege to work for Pastor Dan Sheaffer for those four years. He was a great preacher of

God's Word. I remember one particular sermon he preached on forgiveness. He used a rhyme that I have never forgotten. It was easy to commit to memory. Here it is:

When someone has done you wrong . . .

   a. Don't nurse it.
   b. Don't curse it.
   c. Don't rehearse it.
   d. But disperse it.
   e. God will reverse it!

Don't nurse it. Don't feel sorry for yourself and spend your life licking your wounds.

Don't curse it. Don't talk bad about the person or situation.

Don't rehearse it. Don't keep talking about it over and over again. Let it go — we heard you!

Disperse it. Get rid of all feelings of bitterness and unforgiveness.

God will reverse it. Always remember that God has your back. He can and will honor you for walking in forgiveness.

I had a really eye-opening question asked of me once in a corporate setting. I was attending a Promise Keepers meeting in Nashville, Tennessee, when the speaker said something that I will never forget. "Do you want to be *right,* or do you want to be *reconciled?*" he asked. That question broke me. I decided right then and there that I would rather be reconciled in my relationships than hold out just to prove that

I was right. That day I released a person who had wronged me. Will you do the same?

Whom do you need to forgive today? Do it now!

Questions for Discussion:

1. Describe and discuss the negative side of refusing to forgive. Are there any positives to not forgiving?
2. Do you personally know of relationships that have been destroyed because someone refused to forgive? What happened?
3. Do you have someone you need to forgive? Why haven't you done so?
4. Is there someone who needs to forgive you? Have you made every effort to receive forgiveness from the person?
5. Discuss your thoughts about the following:
   a. Don't nurse it.
   b. Don't curse it.
   c. Don't rehearse it.
   d. But disperse it.
   e. God will reverse it.

MY MARRIAGE IS OVER, SO WHAT NOW?

I am going to ask you some questions. However, in order for this to be a beneficial experience, you need to answer them *honestly*. Okay, ready? Tell the truth now, but have you ever told a lie? Have you ever stolen something? Have you been divorced? Have you failed at something in life? Okay, now, how many of you wish I would shut up and move on?

I know the questions are pointed and revealing. Do you know why it is so hard for us to acknowledge the presence of these kinds of things in our lives? It's because it is painful to admit our failures. It hurts. It is embarrassing.

In this chapter, I want to talk about a certain failure in my life. I want you to learn from my failure and hopefully not make the same mistakes I made. You see, my name is Lynn, and I have been divorced. My first marriage failed—and it was not all her fault. I confess to you that there are some things I could have done differently. I have learned that divorce is not about finger pointing and playing the blame game. That will get you nowhere and will only cause the bitterness to hang on.

I realize that there are several categories of people reading this book. I know some of you have been through a divorce, just like me. I know others of you may be in the process of divorcing, while still others are seriously thinking about it. Some of you have not been through it personally, but you have been touched by divorce because a close friend or family member has been there. While none of these places are good places to be, I will remind you that there is a God who still provides strength to the weak and healing to the broken! As 2 Samuel 22:33 says, "It is God who arms me with strength and makes my way perfect." And Psalm 46:1 reminds us that "God is our refuge and strength, an ever present help in trouble."

My divorce was final in March of 1999. There are some verses in Acts that provide an apt description of how my life was going at that time: "When a gentle south wind began to blow, they thought they had obtained what they wanted, so they weighed anchor and sailed along the shore of Crete. Before very long, a wind of hurricane force, called the 'northeaster,' swept down from the island. The ship was caught by the storm and could not head in to the wind; so we gave way to it and were driven along" (Acts 27:13–15).

Let me share this with you in phases. Just like in those verses, I thought I had obtained what I wanted. Life was good, and the ministry was flourishing.

Then one day I came in from speaking at a ministry event, and the storm hit. This is what happened:

1. FIRST, AN OFFICER KNOCKED ON MY DOOR. He served me with divorce papers. Winds of hurricane force hit me, and my life immediately plunged into a wild, swirling storm like nothing I had ever experienced. Just like some of you would do, I thought, *If I ignore this, it won't really happen.* So I said to the officer, "What happens if I do not respond to this?" The officer replied, "Then you will be taken to jail." I don't know about you, but I will do everything I can to stay out of jail. This initial shock was soon followed by the next step in the process.

2. STRONG EMOTIONS FOLLOWED. They were intense and varied, and I went through all of them. I got scared, nauseated, angry, bitter, lonely, and confused. These emotions repeated themselves often. I also had something else to contend with.

3. OTHERS REACTED TO MY CHANGE IN CIRCUMSTANCE. People spoke their thoughts loud and clear. Some so-called friends deserted me. Pastors and other ministry event leaders began to cancel my speaking engagements. The reactions of others to my divorce brought much confusion and pain.

Jesus Himself had to endure the pain of rejection. Matthew 26:36–43 talks about His journey to Gethsemane with His disciples. This was an intense time in Jesus' life, and He needed prayer support. His disciples, however, kept falling asleep. Even after Jesus pleaded with them to stay awake, they could not. It must have been terrible to feel that heaven was silent and to have your best friends sleep while you struggled. I am in no way comparing what I have been through to what Jesus went through in the Garden of Gethsemane, but I do know that it is very painful when those you thought were your friends let you down.

After the sense of the betrayal came the one thing that almost put me over the edge.

4. AN INCREDIBLE SENSE OF LOSS SET IN. This was overwhelming at times. I went home to an empty apartment with no furniture. I lost my marriage, my income, my ministry, and my self-esteem. This about did me in. This is the thing that eventually drove me to seek counseling.

That moment when you realize the depth of your loss literally takes all the wind out of your sails. This is what urges me to say that if you are on the fence right now and thinking about divorce, try everything you can to work it out. Pray, get help, and do whatever you can to save your marriage.

That was the process I went through. The valley was dark and at times seemed endless, but God was faithful. I wish I could make these next few words ring loud, but the best I can do is put them in print to make my point:

The final authority for our lives is not our friends, our families, or even the church—it is the Word of God! God forgives us of our failures and shortcomings. His grace is sufficient for us all.

Here are some things I want you to know about divorce:

1. DIVORCE DOES NOT DEFINE YOU— GOD DOES!

I think Romans 8:16–17 explains it best: "The Spirit himself testifies with our spirit that we are God's children. Now if we are children, then we are .heirs—heirs of God and co-heirs with Christ, if indeed we share in his sufferings in order that we may also share in his glory." *Being a child of God is what defines you best!* For a couple of years, I felt like everywhere I went, people were talking about my divorce. I felt like I was wearing a shirt with the words *I am divorced* printed on it.

Romans 8:35 says, "Who shall separate us from the love of Christ? Shall trouble or hardship or persecution or famine or nakedness or danger or sword?" Then verse 37 provides the answer: "No, in all these things we are more than conquerors through him who loved us." Not even divorce can separate you from the love of Christ!

If you allow divorce to define you, it will become your crutch. If it becomes your crutch, then it will be your excuse to throw a pity party. You are defined by who your Father is—not by what you have been through.

2. DIVORCE DRAWS YOUR TRUE FRIENDS TOWARD YOU.

Let's look at the reaction of Job's friends when he lost everything. Job 2:11–13 says:

When Job's three friends, Eliphaz the Temanite, Bildad the Shuhite and Zophar the Naamathite, heard about all the troubles that had come upon him, they set out from their homes and met together by agreement to go and sympathize with him and comfort him. When they saw him from a distance, they could hardly recognize him; they began to weep aloud, and they tore their robes and sprinkled dust on their heads. Then they sat on the ground with him for seven days and seven nights. No one said a word to him, because they saw how great his suffering was.

In a crisis like divorce, your true friends will be drawn to you. I had friends who abandoned me, but my true friends drew near to me.

My friend Kevin Ward is the lead pastor at Central Assembly of God in Enid, Oklahoma. At the time of my divorce, Kevin was the youth director for the North Texas district. I will never forget the phone call he made to me right after my divorce was final. He said, "Lynn, I heard what you are going through. I called, but I do not know what to say. I'm sorry I don't know what to say, but I did not want to *not* call." I cried like a little baby at his words. To this day, he has remained a true friend.

Friends and family members of those who are going through difficult things such as divorce need to remember this: it is not *what* you say when you call that makes the difference, but the very fact that you called at all.

I was preaching in Phoenix, Arizona, exactly one month after my divorce was final. I was praying in the afternoon before the evening service that night. I was mentally and emotionally exhausted. I had just told God that I could not do this anymore. I had nothing left to give. Then my phone rang.

It was my friend and colleague, John Davis. John said to me, "Lynn, I was just praying for you, and the Lord wanted me to call and tell you something. Lynn, He wants you to know that there will be friends who walk out on you because of what you are going through, but new friends will walk in during this time. Those that walk in will be stronger than those that walked out." Once again, I cried like a baby.

Over the past thirteen years, that is exactly what has happened. My closest friends today were not even in my life then. Thank God for friends who come near when you need them!

3. DIVORCE REQUIRES THE HEALING OF A SUPERNATURAL GOD.

God has promised not only to be with you, but also to heal you. Jeremiah 30:17 says, " 'But I will restore you to health and heal your wounds,' declares the Lord." I also love the promise of Psalm 147:3: "He heals the brokenhearted and binds up their wounds."

Your friends, pastor, church, and family can all help to a degree, but this kind of wound requires God to get involved—it requires His healing. He can bring a level of healing that no friend or family member can bring. He can restore you to health like no church or pastor can do. Recovering from divorce requires the healing of a supernatural God.

Some people relish in our failures, but Christ redeems us from our failures!

4. DIVORCE CAN KNOCK YOU DOWN, BUT IT CANNOT KEEP YOU DOWN.

Philippians 3:13–14 says, "Brothers, I do not consider myself yet to have taken hold of it. But one thing I do: Forgetting what is behind and straining toward what is ahead, I press on toward the goal to win the prize for which God has called me heavenward in Christ Jesus."

I am so humbled and broken to report to you the restoring power of God in my life. At the time of this writing—and since my divorce—over 3,500 people have come to know the Lord in my ministry events. Divorce knocked me down, but it did not keep me down. *God is faithful!*

Also, I am about to celebrate my sixth anniversary with the love of my life, Dianna. She was a godsend at just the right time. God heals and restores, so keep pressing forward.

You may be asking, "How does God feel about all this?" Well, Scripture is very clear: God hates divorce (Mal. 2:16). I want you to know that I, too, hate divorce. I lived through it and survived, but I have seen the devastating and lasting affects of it.

You may be saying, "Well, you made it okay, so I will be fine too." Think about that, friend. You have no guarantees of how things will work out for you.

Still others of you may be thinking that the grass is greener on the other side. Warning: That is Astro

Turf! It is not real. Do not buy in to that lie from the enemy.

For those of you whose marriage is already over, you may be wondering what comes next. Here are three things I want to encourage you to do:

1. STAY FAITHFUL TO GOD. Do not think about quitting God or the church. Stay faithful. He is still your answer.
2. DRAW STRENGTH FROM GOD. Pursue Him and He will strengthen you daily.
3. TRUST THAT GOD WILL BRING YOU THROUGH. Keep the faith. Let the joy of the Lord be your strength (Neh. 8:10). He is no respecter of persons. What He has done for me, He will do for you.

Get up every morning and recite these three things, if you need to. Say them over and over again. Hold your head up, child of God. You may be divorced, but you are not done! God still wants to use you. What the devil intended for bad, God will turn for the good. Trust Him!

Questions for Discussion:

1. Have you ever helped a friend or family member get through a divorce? What did you do?
2. Why do you think people have a tendency to treat other people differently or even discontinue a friendship after a person is divorced?

3. Have you been through a divorce? What were the key factors that helped you get through it?
4. Why does it seem so hard to receive healing for the emotional pain of broken relationships?
5. Why do you think that the divorce rate in America continues to rise? Is there anything we can do to reverse this trend?

STICKS AND STONES

*W*e all have something in common: we have all said things we wish we could take back. Several times in my life, before the words I spoke even got past my mustache, I have wanted to reach out and grab them and put them back in. It is a horrible feeling and an awkward moment when words that you regret come out of your mouth.

On the other hand, we have also had words spoken to us that were very hurtful. We have been called names or criticized, and it cut deep. Such words can leave deep wounds that take years to heal, if they ever do. If you have been through a relational disaster of any kind, chances are good that you are very much in touch with what I am saying right now. Criticism and derogatory remarks directed toward us are not easily forgotten. As I am writing this chapter, I am praying that my words will minister to you and bring healing to issues that have lodged deep in your spirit.

Nobody likes to be around complaining, critical people. I recently boarded a plane and was just getting comfortable when a certain woman sat in the seat right across the aisle from me. As soon as she sat down, I knew it was going to be a long flight.

The woman started in immediately with her complaints: "This seat is uncomfortable; this is a lousy airline." Then she was cold, so the flight attendant brought her a blanket, to which she responded, "This blanket stinks; this is a lousy airline." She wanted to read, but complained, "There isn't enough light on this plane; this is a lousy airline." The attendants brought her some coffee, and she said, "This tastes terrible; this is a lousy airline." You get the picture. Everything anyone tried to do to make her happy and comfortable, she criticized.

I don't mind telling you that after a few minutes of that, I wanted to ask that woman to step outside. Yes, I know we were thirty thousand feet in the air!

In my ministry office, we receive many positive, uplifting, and encouraging reports. But there are also times when we get some negative feedback. It can be a hundred positive testimonies to only one negative, critical remark, but I have a tendency to focus on that one.

Why do we tend to focus on the one instead of the one hundred? We can recite repeatedly the words we learned as kids, "Sticks and stones may break my bones, but words will never hurt me"; but in reality, that is not true. Words do hurt. The pain they cause does not vanish quickly.

Some people have had their lives drastically altered because someone spoke critical words to them in a condescending manner. It crushed their dreams and altered their course of life. If that is you, my prayer is that *today* the healing process will begin.

Have you ever been criticized for an honest mistake? I have. I grew up in Oklahoma City, Oklahoma, and we had a Mexican restaurant called Pancho's. As a teenager, I went to work there. After a few months, I worked my way up and became a waiter.

Pancho's sported little flags on each of the tables, and when the customers wanted more food, they would raise their flags to signal the wait staff to come over and get their requests for whatever they wanted. I had just become a waiter, and it was a very busy Friday night. A group of people at one of the tables raised their flag, and when I got to them, the man said he wanted an "enchilada, beef." I *thought* he said he wanted " a lot of beans."

I thought the request was a bit odd, but I went to the kitchen and piled on the beans. When I brought the plate to the table, the man was livid. He started yelling at me and calling me names. I was the worst waiter he had ever had, he said. I had made an honest mistake and simply misheard the gentleman. He let me have it with both barrels, though, and nothing I said could persuade him to let up.

Then there are other times when we keep talking though we should just hush. My wife, Dianna, fixes the best Parmesan chicken in the world. I love it, and she knows I love it. Once when she made it for me, she asked me how it was. I said, "It's good. It was better last time, but it's good." (Every woman reading this right now wants to smack me one!) I know, I should have stopped with "it's good." I saw the hurt on her face as soon as I said it. I apologized, but it was a lesson learned. Sometimes when you are in a hole, you need to quit digging.

This chapter is going to contain four power points concerning criticism. The first two will discuss the dangers of being critical. The last two will help us learn how to handle criticism directed against us. The purpose of these four points is twofold. First of all, the next time we start to be critical, we need to remember to simply hush. Second, we all must realize that God is a more powerful force in our lives than any critical words spoken to us.

Consider these thoughts from Scripture:

"The tongue has the power of life and death, and those who love it will eat its fruit" (Prov. 18:21).

"If anyone considers himself religious and yet does not keep a tight rein on his tongue, he deceives himself and his religion is worthless" (James 1:26).

"Do not let any unwholesome talk come out of your mouth, but only what is helpful for building others up according to their needs, that it may benefit those who listen" (Eph. 4:29).

Most critical people are like teeter-totters: they put others down to lift themselves up!

Here are the four power points to remember about criticism:

1. IT IS A MATTER OF THE HEART.

"The good man brings good things out of the good stored up in his heart, and the evil man brings evil things out of the evil stored up in his heart. For out of the overflow of his heart, his mouth speaks" (Luke 6:45).

Criticism is more than what we speak or think; it is a matter of the heart.

I am an avid coffee drinker. I'm sure I will have Starbucks in my mansion in heaven! When you want to make coffee, you need a few things in order to successfully brew a delicious cup of the drink. If you pour water into the coffeemaker and then put the coffee into the filter basket, you will end up with coffee grounds in your cup. Yuck! Nobody likes that. The only thing that will prevent that is the use of a filter to keep the junk out of your coffee.

If you have a tender heart for God, it can act as your filter. You can process all your words through your heart and allow it to filter out the critical ones.

Remember the words of Zig Ziglar: "When you throw dirt at people, you are only losing ground," and the words of Winston Churchill: "Nobody has ever harmed their stomach by swallowing harmful words left unsaid."

2. CRITICISM EVENTUALLY BRINGS NEGATIVE RESULTS.

The result of criticism will eventually be division. It will eventually divide the workplace, the church, or the family where it is allowed to spread its influence.

Sometimes people try to cover up their criticism by framing it as a joke. Maybe someone made a jab at you in front of others, and everyone else laughed, but the comment hurt you deeply. We have all been on the receiving end of those kinds of sarcastic, critical jabs. Friend, criticism framed as a joke is still criticism. We would all do well to remember Ephesians 5:4: "Nor should there be obscenity, foolish talk or coarse joking, which are out of place, but rather thanksgiving."

Do not let unjust criticism stop what God is doing in your life! With that said, I now want to try to help you handle criticism that comes your way.

3. REMEMBER THAT CRITICAL PEOPLE USUALLY DO NOT HAVE ALL THE FACTS.

Nehemiah 4:1–3 reads:

> When Sanballat heard that we were rebuilding the wall, he became angry and greatly incensed. He ridiculed the Jews, and in the presence of his associates and the army of Samaria he said, "What are those feeble

Jews doing? Will they restore their wall? Will they offer sacrifices? Will they finish in a day? Can they bring the stones back to life from those heaps of rubbles—burned as they are?"

Tobiah, the Ammonite, who was at his side said, "What are they building—if even a fox climbed up on it, he would break down their wall of stones!"

Nehemiah and his men were trying to do good in their effort to rebuild the walls of Jerusalem. With permission from the king, they forged ahead, only to have a group of men begin to criticize them and even call them names. These men mocked and made fun of Nehemiah and his men, but they did not have all the facts. They were not on the leadership team, nor had they been in the meeting between Nehemiah and the king. Despite their limited knowledge of the true facts, they criticized.

People who criticize you or something you have done usually don't have all the facts. Nevertheless, some people will hurt you with critical words even though your motives are pure and you are trying to do good.

Here is something I once heard a preacher use years ago. It helped me so much that I memorized it. I hope it helps you too. When people criticize you or set out to harm you, let me remind you of what I shared in the chapter on forgiveness:

Don't nurse it (act wounded all the time).
Don't curse it.
Don't rehearse it (talk about it all the time).
But disperse it.
God will reverse it!

Isaiah 34:8 says it clearly: "For the Lord has a day of vengeance, a year of retribution to uphold Zion's cause."

Those five things mentioned above apply to the area of undeserved criticism. I want to encourage you to memorize them and make them action steps in your life.

4. CRITICISM IS JUST ONE PERSON'S OPINION.

"Peter and the other apostles replied, 'We must obey God rather than men' " (Acts 5:29).

"Am I now trying to win the approval of men, or God? Am I trying to please men? If I were trying to please men, I would not be a servant of Christ" (Gal. 1:10).

These two verses clearly tell us that the most important thing in our lives is to please God. Those hurtful, harmful words that were directed at you were just one person's opinion. Those words and the people who said them are not the deciding vote of your life — *God is!*

A few years ago, I wanted to take my wife to a nice place on Valentine's Day. Several times we had talked about wanting to eat at a particular restaurant in Tulsa, so I got us a reservation there. I was excited and hoping it would be a nice evening for us.

The night before our dinner, we decided to go online and look at their menu. It looked great. However, we noticed a tab to click to read reviews of the restaurant. We clicked it with great confidence, knowing this was going to be a great evening for us. The first review that came up said, "Lousy food and service." My heart sank. Oops! We had already driven to Tulsa, and we were committed. We went to the restaurant anyway, and guess what? We had great food and great service! We had an awesome time in a great atmosphere.

You see, sometimes one person's opinion is not reality. It is only *their opinion.*

I always love it when people approach me with these words: "Let me give you some *constructive* criticism." Usually, it is not very constructive; it merely provides an opportunity for them to air their opinions. They make it sound like *everybody* feels this way and agrees with them. Funny, though, when I ask for specific names, they never can come up with any.

Constructive criticism is when I criticize you. Destructive criticism is when you criticize me. That's generally how we think, isn't it?

In your efforts to move past any relational disaster in your life, remember to hold your tongue and believe that God is still working on you. What

God says about you is more important than what anyone else says or thinks. Believe it!

Questions for Discussion:

1. How do you respond when criticized? Why do you react that way?
2. Is there ever a time when criticism is inappropriate? If so, discuss when and under what circumstances.
3. Is there really such a thing as constructive criticism? Has it ever had a positive effect on you?
4. On a scale of 1 to 10 (with 10 representing the highest value) how much does it matter to you what people think of you? Would you consider that a healthy number?
5. Have you ever been critical and harsh with your words and knew that you had hurt someone, but did nothing to make it right? Is there anyone to whom you owe an apology? If so, who is it, and will you make it right?

MIRACLE ON THE OTHER SIDE

I want to acknowledge the desperation in many of you who may be reading this book right now. I want you to know that I understand your longing for God to move on your behalf, because I have been there. In short, I understand that you need a miracle!

My definition of a miracle is this: something that requires God to get involved. It is something that will not happen unless God gets involved. Your friends, family, church, pastor, and other people cannot do it for you. It requires God, or it will not get done.

For those of you who need a miracle on the other side of courageous, I want to remind you that God is still a miracle-working God. I do not want to sound old-fashioned here or even sound like I am just repeating clichés from gifted communicators, but with all my heart I truly believe that God still performs miracles and can do one for you.

Your family situation may look like it is beyond repair. Your failure may have caused you to feel like you will never bounce back. Your broken heart may feel like it can never be healed. There are so many needs in the body of Christ today, and yours is but one.

I want to pray something over you right now. Even while I am writing this, I am praying for every person who needs God *now*. I want to pray a twenty-four-hour turnaround over you! I pray that what you are feeling or facing today will be gone in the next twenty-four hours. It is a scriptural prayer, and I am believing it for you!

In 2 Kings 7:1–2, the Word of God says:

> Elisha said, "Hear the word of the Lord. This is what the Lord says: About this time tomorrow, a seah of flour will sell for a shekel and two seahs of barley for a shekel at the gate of Samaria."

> The officer on whose arm the king was leaning said to the man of God, "Look, even if the Lord should open the floodgates of the heavens, could this happen?"

> "You will see it with your own eyes," answered Elisha, "but you will not eat any of it."

Focus on the phrase in verse 1 "about this time tomorrow." In Scripture, the Lord spoke in this manner on more than one occasion. In other places,

He sometimes said "by this time next year." He often put a time limit on a need. By doing so when we pray, we are simply agreeing out loud with God. I am praying a twenty-four-hour turnaround in your life and situation, that what you see today, you will not see tomorrow. I am encouraging you to declare it with me in your life.

From 1985–1989, I served as a youth pastor at Crossroads Church in Oklahoma City, Oklahoma. Our offices were in a separate building from our sanctuary. All the staff offices were located in the same place as most of the classrooms, the fellowship area, and the kitchen.

Every year our church hosted a big craft fair. People would come from all over Oklahoma City and set up tables to sell different products. The best place to hold the event was in the fellowship area, which, unfortunately, was also where our offices were located. Most of the ministry team would work behind closed doors during that time. The noise level was high, but we were team players and coped as best we could.

Well, you can never have a craft fair without also having food. You have to have it! The ladies would make brownies, pies, cookies, cupcakes, etc. You name it, and it was there. From our offices, we could smell all these delicacies. My office was located right next door to the office of the associate pastor at that time, Gary Bohanon. Gary and I would frequently discuss the delicious aromas of the various desserts.

One year I was in my office doing my youth pastor thing. It was during the craft fair, so I had my door closed. All of a sudden, a knock sounded at my door, so I said, "Come in." In walked a couple of my students carrying brownies and chocolate-chip cookies. Yummy! I was surprised and delighted at their thoughtfulness. I finished the treats quickly and went back to working.

About thirty minutes later, another knock sounded at my door. More cookies! It was a good day in my life. The process repeated itself one more time, and I was enjoying immensely my students acting as my waiters and waitresses. I was thinking this would continue all day, but I was wrong. Suddenly it all stopped.

After a few minutes, my curiosity was piqued. Then, after an hour, I began to wonder what had happened to all the students with my food. Finally, I left my office to go find them and get my parade of brownies started again. As soon as I walked out of my office, I realized what had happened. I opened my door to discover that someone had posted a sign on it that said, "Please *do not* feed the animals!"

I knew immediately where the sign had come from. I walked to the office next door and knocked. As soon as I knocked, I could hear laughter from inside the office. I walked in and threw the sign on the desk of our beloved associate pastor and declared his actions "not from God."

When we are enjoying something and it stops, we want to know why. We also want to know what we can do to get it started again. I feel the same way about miracles. If they have stopped in your life and church, let's find out why, correct the problem, and get them going again. On the other side of coura-geous, we are desperate for miracles.

If you go back to 2 Kings 6:25, you will discover what prompted Elisha's prophecy. The Bible says, "There was a great famine in the land." This famine affected the economy in a big way. It was like a modern-day stock-market crash. It lessened the value of everything, including currency.

Let's divide this prophecy into two categories. Let's look at what happened before the prophecy and what happened after the prophecy in 2 Kings 7:1–2. Notice the following:

1. BEFORE THE PROPHECY

   a. Recognition of desperation—In 2 Kings 6:26, we read, "As the king of Israel was passing by on the wall, a woman cried to him, 'Help me, my lord the king!'" People in the city became so desperate that they began to cry out for help.

Some of you reading this right now have some very desperate situations in your life. I want to encourage you with these words: be desperate for your Savior, not about your situation! Get desperate for God, and your situation will work out. Blind Bartimaeus was desperate when he cried out to Jesus in Mark 10:46, "Jesus, Son of David, have mercy on me!" Friend, cry out to Him today. He is the master of the twenty-four-hour turnaround.

b. Recognition of a lack of resources—In 2 Kings 6:27, we see the king's response to the woman: "The king replied, 'If the Lord does not help, where can I get help for you? From the threshing floor? From the winepress?' "

The king was basically saying there was nowhere for him to get help for the woman. Even the threshing floors and winepresses were empty. When there is a lack of resources, not even the king of Israel can help you!

c. Recognition of inadequacy—The story goes on in verses 28–29 to talk about women killing their children in order to eat their flesh. I think this illustrates how desperate the time was. The king could offer no help of any kind.

It is important to remember that *that* king is not *your* King! The king of Israel, with all of his authority, could not do anything for these people, but our King never runs out of resources. He can and will respond to us in desperate times on the other side of courageous. When we are weak, He is strong. We must decrease so that He can increase.

2. AFTER THE PROPHECY

a. Those that miss the harvest, or miracle— The officer contradicted Elisha's prophecy and thus missed the harvest. In 2 Kings 7:2, the Bible says, "You will see it with your own eyes," answered Elisha, " but you will not eat any of it." It was true. This man's death is recorded in verse 17. He saw it, but did not taste it. I do not want an unbelieving attitude or words to stop me from receiving my miracle.

b. Those that reap the harvest—A group of lepers reaped the harvest in 2 Kings 7:3–9. If you have not read my book *The F.O.G. is Rolling In*, I encourage you to do so. There is a chapter called "Lessons from Lepers" that will minister to you in a powerful way.

There are two things in particular the Lord wants me to share with you regarding your miracle and your twenty-four-hour turnaround:

1. Things in you will live again! So many on the other side of courageous have been through broken relationships that make them feel like rejects. For others, their dreams have died and need to be resurrected. Know that your dreams will live again. Just like Elisha stretched himself over a boy who was dead and spoke life into him (read 2 Kings 4), I speak life back into your dreams. You thought your life had been derailed, but it was only a detour. You and your dreams will live again!

2. Things will be restored to you! Second Kings 8:1–6 tells a great story of restoration. I will tell it to you, but I encourage you to read it for yourself.

The same lady whose son Elisha had raised from the dead left the country for seven years during the famine. When someone departed in that fashion, the government could take their land and house, which is what happened in this woman's case. After seven years, the woman returned home and approached the king about getting her house and her land back. That is all she wanted. The famine was over, and she was back. Her request was to regain her land and a place to live so that she could work for a harvest.

The king consulted with some of those close to him. After talking with them, he granted the woman her land and her house. How wonderful! God is indeed a restoring God. But wait, there's more! The king also granted the woman seven years' worth of lost income. Seven years' worth of wages! How would you like to receive a check right now for seven years' worth of wages? The woman did not even ask for that, but the king gave it to her anyway. Yes, God is a restoring God. Sometimes He even restores beyond our request. I love when that happens!

It is my prayer that those dreams that have died within you will be resurrected and that things that have been lost or taken from you will be restored. I pray for restoration beyond your request. A twenty-four-hour turnaround—God can do that, even on the other side of courageous!

Questions for Discussion:

1. Has God ever done a miracle for you? Please share.
2. Why do you think we do not see miracles in public worship services like we used to?
3. Do you have a story of a miracle of restoration, relational or otherwise? Please share.
4. Why does it seem so much harder to pursue God when you are desperate for a miracle? Have you ever experienced that? Share what happened.
5. How often do you pray specifically for miracles, both privately and publicly?

GRACE ON
THE OTHER SIDE

G ood news! The grace of God covers you on the other side of courageous.

Where would we be without His grace? We not only needed His grace the day we gave our hearts to God and became Christ-followers, but we also need His grace every day of our lives. There is nothing that I am more thankful for than the grace of God. I am not yet what I want to be, but by His grace, I am not what I was. I am thankful for that. How about you?

We are on the other side of where we want to be right now for different reasons. Some reading this book are there because of someone else's bad decisions or inconsiderateness. Maybe some of you are there because someone lied to you or deceived you. Perhaps some are there because of their own bad choices, wrong actions, and even sins.

But the good news is that God's grace covers it all. Regardless of why you are where you are today,

His grace is sufficient for you! His grace not only redeems you from your sins, but also from your failures and bad choices. Even if others have not forgiven you, I encourage you to move forward today in His grace.

In Acts 11, a move of God broke out in Antioch, and the church at Jerusalem sent Barnabas to check it out. In Acts 11:23, the Bible tells us, "When he arrived and saw the evidence of the grace of God." He *saw* the evidence of grace! That verse brings two questions to my mind: First of all, has anybody actually seen grace? And second, what does grace look like?

If Barnabas saw it—and the Word says he did—what did it look like? Does grace look like the image I present to the world? I want to be known as an individual of grace. I have received grace, and I want to extend grace. How about you?

Does the church project a clear picture of grace? I believe that every church should strive to be a grace place. I want more than illustrated sermons, cutting-edge programs, and awesome worship. I love all those things, but if we have all that and no grace, we are lacking. May the Lord take us past rut, ritual, and routine to an extension of His grace to others.

As Barnabas continued his journey through Acts 11, we can see some evidences of the grace of God:

1. WHEN GRACE IS PRESENT, PEOPLE TURN TO THE LORD.

The first evidence that the grace of God is working is that people's hearts turn to the Lord. That actually is recorded in two different verses in Acts 11. First, verse 21 says, "The Lord's hand was with them, and a great number of people believed and turned to the Lord." And verse 24 says, "He was a good man, full of the Holy Spirit and faith, and a great number of people were brought to the Lord."

As a traveling minister for the past twenty-six years, I have seen some radical life changes in many people, and I always rejoice in that. After all, a changed life is recognition of the grace of God. However, we not only need God's grace the moment we accept Him in our heart, but we also need God's grace every day of our life. We will never not need His grace. We are who we are and what we are only because of His grace!

I am convinced that the evidence here was not intended only for the people who were giving their hearts to God for the first time, but also for the believers. You see, even as Christ-followers, we sometimes get our priorities out of line and allow other things to become too important. In the busyness of life, it is easy for that to happen. The evidence of grace should not be found only in new believers, but in all of us who follow Christ. My prayer is that we would all turn our hearts toward Him and make Him our number one priority.

If you are struggling with misaligned priorities today, I encourage you to realign them now. God has to be number one, or you open yourself to all kinds of chaos in your life.

James 4:17 says, "For it is time for judgment to begin with the family of God; and if it begins with us, what will the outcome be for those who do not obey the gospel of God?" I am so thankful for God's grace on both sides of courageous!

2. GRACE HAS A REPUTATION.

The second thing I want you to know is that grace has a reputation. Acts 11:22 says, "News of this reached the ears of the church at Jerusalem, and they sent Barnabas to Antioch." Please focus on the words "news of this reached the ears of the church at Jerusalem." The word got out. Lives were being changed by the grace of God. Whenever that happens, word gets out! People begin to talk, and grace develops a reputation.

Grace still has a reputation today. When churches have their weekly worship experiences, a net should always be cast for grace to do its work. I believe an opportunity for people to find Christ is imperative when we meet together. I know of churches that see over a hundred people saved on a weekly basis. However, the number is not what brings value to the net. If only one person accepts the Lord in that public gathering, it was worth casting the net for that one. Jesus often stopped for one person, altering His course for that one. He always placed high value on one.

Matthew 18:12–14 says, "What do you think? If a man owns a hundred sheep, and one of them wanders away, will he not leave the ninety-nine on the hills and go look for the one who wandered off? And if he finds it, I tell you the truth, he is happier about that one sheep than about the ninety-nine that did not wander off. In the same way your Father in heaven is not willing that any of these little ones should be lost."

Grace not only saves in masses in public meetings, but it also works in personal evangelism. Living the Christian life before the lost and sharing the gospel one-on-one is still a commandment from Christ for us to follow.

There have been a number of times when I lay in my hotel room exhausted and wondering where I would get the strength to minister. Then grace showed up and empowered me. His grace saved us and is still strong enough to carry us through. What a reputation grace has!

3. GRACE LEAVES EVIDENCE BEHIND.

Webster's Dictionary says that *evidence* is a "sign; something that tends to prove."

As I read through Scripture, I see the evidence of God's grace at work in several people's lives. The Samaritan woman found grace at a well (John 4). This is a great illustration of a woman on the other side of courageous. By all indications, she had searched for happiness and fulfillment through relationships, and that had failed her. Jesus said to her in verses 17–18, "You are right when you say you have no husband. The fact is, you have had five husbands, and the man you now have is not your husband. What you have said is quite true."

However, at that well, Jesus did not judge her. He did not walk through her life with her and tell her everything she had done wrong. He simply extended grace on the other side of courageous. A broken, hurting woman was changed by God's grace, and it was evident. In verses 28–29, the Bible records, "Then, leaving her water jar, the woman went back to the town and said to the people, 'Come, see a man who told me everything I did. Could this be the Christ?'"

Later in that chapter, the Bible says, "Many of the Samaritans from that town believed in him because of the woman's testimony, 'He told me everything I did'" (John 4:39). Life change!

There are so many lives in Scripture that were changed by the grace of God. I not only see it in Scripture, but I see it everywhere I go. People's lives have been changed by the grace of God, and the evidence is there. They do not act like they used to act or talk like they used to talk. Attitudes are different, and servanthood is priority now. These are lives changed because of the grace of God.

Some of you reading this are a product of the grace of God, and it is evident. The enemy of your soul gave his best shot to destroy you, your family, your health, and your finances, but you survived.

By the grace of God, you are still here and serving Christ. You have only to look in the mirror to see the evidence of God's grace. Now you are not just surviving, but you are thriving *by the grace of God*.

4. GRACE HUMBLES YOU.

Acts 11:25–26 says, "Then Barnabas went to Tarsus to look for Saul, and when he found him, he brought him to Antioch. So for a whole year Barnabas and Saul met with the church and taught great numbers of people. The disciples were called Christians first at Antioch."

This is such an important lesson to learn on either side of courageous. Remember that Saul's conversion was relatively new (see Acts 9). Prior to his conversion, he was a persecutor of the Christians. He had been a thorn in their side for years. Chances are, he criticized Barnabas and others in church leadership in Jerusalem. He gave them fits.

However, now that this move of God had broken out, Barnabas wanted Saul to be a part of it. He was never ordered by the church leadership to do so, but he humbled himself and went to get Saul. Saul, the man who had persecuted him, was now working alongside him in ministry. Grace brings a new level of humility to us all. If ever we start to get puffed up with pride, let us remember we are who we are only by the grace of God.

Just like Barnabas and Saul needed grace to get past their differences and work together for a year, we need that grace as well with some of the people we know. Think about the person who lied about you or the one who told you they loved you, but then walked away. Then there are those people who intentionally meant to harm you. We all have those people we struggle with, the ones whose very names make us cringe. The Bible says we are to pray for them, but honestly, most of us pray we don't have to cross paths with them ever again or that they will quit making us mad!

If we are honest, we will admit that we feel as though we have run out of grace with certain people. They have crossed a line or used up all their forgiveness points with us. James talked about that when he said, "But he gives us more grace" (James 4:6). That is good news! When we run out of grace, Christ will give us more grace—grace to handle people or situations that are less than desirable. Whatever you are going through today, He will give you the grace to handle it. His grace is sufficient for you: "My grace is sufficient for you, for my power is made perfect in weakness" (2 Cor. 12:9).

Jesus tells an incredible story of grace in Luke 15:11–24. This is a story about a man who ended up on the other side of courageous. Read what the Bible says:

> There was a man who had two sons. The younger one said to his father, "Father, give me my share of the estate." So he divided his property between them.
>
> Not long after that, the younger son got together all he had, set off for a distant country

and there squandered his wealth in wild living. After he had spent everything, there was a severe famine in that whole country, and he began to be in need. So he went and hired himself out to a citizen of that country, who sent him to his fields to feed pigs. He longed to fill his stomach with the pods that the pigs were eating, but no one gave him anything.

When he came to his senses, he said, "How many of my fathers hired men have food to spare, and here I am starving to death! I will set out and go back to my father and say to him: Father, I have sinned against heaven and against you. I am no longer worthy to be called your son; make me like one of your hired men." So he got up and went to his father.

But while he was still a long way off, his father saw him and had compassion on him; he ran to his son, threw his arms around him and kissed him.

The son said to him, "Father, I have sinned against heaven and against you. I am no longer worthy to be called your son."

But the father said to his servants, "Quick! Bring the best robe and put it on him. Put a ring on his finger and sandals on his feet. Bring the fattened calf and kill it. Let's have a feast and celebrate. For this son of mine was dead and is alive again; he was lost and is found." So they began to celebrate.

What an incredible story of grace extended by a father to his son! The prodigal son, humbled and broken, started for home wondering what would be waiting for him. *Will my dad start yelling at me for my poor decisions? Will he take me back? Can he ever forgive me?*

I love the part that says "his father saw him . . . and ran to his son." Grace was waiting on him. Grace served as a bridge to get him from one side of courageous to the other. I have needed that bridge and will need that bridge again, I'm sure. Please know that bridge is there for you today. God loves you, no matter what!

Questions for Discussion:

1. Do you believe you can see when the grace of God has worked in somebody's life? Describe what it looks like.
2. Have you needed God's grace in the last week? On what day did you need it, and why did you need His grace?
3. In the story of the prodigal son, how does the father remind you of your heavenly Father? What differences are there between the two?
4. Does God ever run out of grace? Do we? Discuss.
5. How does grace play a role in our everyday lives?

SIR,
YOUR TABLE IS READY

*T*his year (2012), I celebrated thirty years of full-time ministry. Of those thirty years, I have spent twenty-six as a traveling minister. I have seen a lot of things come and go and then come back again. Changes in church culture and in our society have brought changes to my ministry. We all learn to adjust and adapt in our callings, and I have had to do that too. I am not complaining, just explaining.

One of the things that has been a constant in my life is that I have always eaten out a lot. I have, by far, had more meals at restaurants than in my own home. Again, I am not complaining; I actually enjoy that. People always ask me if I get tired of it, but to me, it is just a part of what I do. Besides, who doesn't like to eat!

One of the things that has changed in restaurants over the last decade is the beeper many restaurants give you when a table is not yet available. You get your name on a list, and then you are buzzed when your table is ready. I guess that says a lot about our society. We would rather push a button to inform someone that their table is ready than walk ten steps to tell them personally. I think people just like pushing buttons and playing with gadgets.

For most of the ministry events where I speak, I fly into a city on Saturday evening to prepare for ministry on Sunday. After the flight, I usually enjoy a great time of fellowship with the pastor or another ministry leader before I am taken to my hotel. That fellowship *always* includes food. It seems those of us in ministry can always solve the world's problems better if food is included in the discussion.

One of the things we can usually count on is a crowded restaurant. In most places, Saturday night means restaurants are jam-packed with people. That usually means a time of waiting before we are seated. After a long travel day, I am always ready for the words "Sir, your table is ready." The waiting process is over, and now the war is on—man versus food.

Those words, "Sir, your table is ready," indicate two things: First of all, my wait is over—yes! Second, I am now about to enjoy a meal—yes, yes! Needless to say, those words are like music to my ears. Even if you have been notified by buzzer, when you take the buzzer to the person, you get to hear those glorious words.

For many of you who have been on the other side of courageous, life has been a long period of separation and isolation from hopes and dreams that have been shattered and scattered. Some of this was due to your own bad choices, and some was due to others' decisions. Regardless, you have felt isolated and alone, feeling as though nobody understands or even cares.

There is a great story in Scripture that has helped me through times like that in my life, and prayerfully it will help you too. The story is about a man named Mephibosheth, and it is found in 2 Samuel 9:1–13:

> David asked, "Is there anyone still left of the house of Saul to whom I can show kindness for Jonathan's sake?
>
> Now there was a servant of Saul's household named Ziba. They called him to appear before David, and the king said to him, "Are you Ziba?"
>
> "Your servant," he replied.
>
> The king asked, "Is there no one still left of the house of Saul to whom I can show God's kindness?"
>
> Ziba answered the king, "There is still a son of Jonathan; he is crippled in both feet."
>
> "Where is he?" the king asked.
>
> Ziba answered, "He is at the house of Makir son of Ammiel in Lo Debar."
>
> So King David had him brought from Lo Debar, from the house of Makir son of Ammiel.
>
> When Mephibosheth son of Jonathan, the son of Saul, came to David, he bowed down to pay him honor.
>
> David said, "Mephibosheth!"
>
> "Your servant," he replied.
>
> "Don't be afraid," David said to him, "for I will surely show you kindness for the sake of

your father Jonathan. I will restore to you all the land that belonged to your grandfather Saul, and you will always eat at my table."

Mephibosheth bowed down and said, "What is your servant that you should notice a dead dog like me?"

Then the king summoned Ziba, Saul's servant, and said to him, "I have given your master's grandson everything that belonged to Saul and his family. You and your sons and your servants are to farm the land for him and bring in the crops, so that your master's grandson may be provided for. And Mephibosheth, grandson of your master, will always eat at my table." (Now Ziba had fifteen sons and twenty servants.)

Then Ziba said to the king, "Your servant will do whatever the lord my king commands his servant to do." So Mephibosheth ate at David's table like one of the king's sons.

Mephibosheth had a young son named Mica, and all the members of Ziba's household were servants of Mephibosheth. And Mephibosheth lived in Jerusalem, because he always ate at the king's table, and he was crippled in both feet.

Let's look at this man Mephibosheth. At this point in his life, he was definitely on the other side of courageous.

1. THE PERSON HE WAS

First of all, let's look at the person he was. He was a man born into royalty. Saul, his grandfather, had been king. Jonathan, his father, had been the prince. From the moment he was born, life looked good for Mephibosheth. He was born with a silver spoon in his mouth, so to speak, The way it looked, he would never want for anything.

Then, in one battle, he lost it all. In the battle on Mount Gilboa (see 1 Samuel 31:1), both his father and grandfather were killed. One battle, one moment, one bad decision, one wrong choice changed everything in his life and future. Maybe that is where you are today. One moment has changed everything in your life too.

Let's look at what happened next. One bullet in one battle changed his life and destiny forever. When the news came that both Mephibosheth's father and grandfather had perished, a nurse hurriedly swept the five-year-old child into her arms. In her haste to flee, she accidentally dropped him, and he became crippled in both feet because of the fall (2 Sam. 4:4). In a short time, Mephibosheth went from being royalty in line to be king to being a cripple in exile. The sad thing is he was only five years old when he lost his father and grandfather and became crippled.

It was nobody's fault that the child was crippled. It was an accident. Yet Mephibosheth still ended up on the other side of courageous. We have all experienced this in one way or another—the *drop*, the *fall*, and then the *crippling*. Whether through despair, depression, the death of a loved one, divorce papers being served, bankruptcy, or some other trauma, we have all fallen into confusion, bondage, or even sin. We have found ourselves dropped into a place where we never thought we would be and do not belong — a place very unfamiliar. Life goes on . . . and we wish our table was ready.

2. THE PLACE HE WAS

Mephibosheth ended up in a place called Lo Debar, a city east of the Jordan River. This city was characterized by barrenness and wastelands. It was a city in the midst of a wilderness, a place of no pasture and no greenery, a place of desolation. The isolation on the other side of courageous is always devastating.

Mephibosheth lost his rank, respectability, reputation, superiority, and self-will. He went from living in a palace to hiding out with a family friend, from being a prince to living as a servant. Over the years, his place of power turned into a place of fear. His self-image was shattered, and he referred to himself as a "dead dog." Interestingly, Mephibosheth's name actually means "scatters shame."

I remember isolating myself when I was broken. I remember the loneliness and depression that came with isolation. Few sought me out. I can tell you, it was the worst of times for me. I struggled mentally and emotionally like never before. I wondered if anybody even cared or if my table would ever be ready.

Maybe you can relate to Mephibosheth and me. Maybe you feel like you are in a dry, barren place right now. Do you feel like you have lost your respect-ability and self-will? Well, there is good news: Christ has a reputation of showing up during the dry times. He is on His way, but until then, you probably sure wish your table was ready.

Psalm 42:2 beautifully expresses this feeling of isolation and longing: "My soul thirsts for God, for the living God. When can I go and meet with God?"

3. THE PLACE HE WAS GOING

The Lord can find us on the other side of the desert. We may feel dry and barren with no hope for the future, but He sees us as part of His family. He found Mephibosheth, and he will find you. Let's see what happened in our story.

David wanted to honor his fallen friend, Jonathan. He simply asked the question "Is there nobody left in his household that I can honor?" Someone knew about Mephibosheth, and when they told the king, the king sent for him. Surprised that anyone, espe-cially the king, would want anything to do with him, Mephibosheth was nonetheless summoned to the king's house. He was twenty years old. After fifteen years in dry, desolate Lo Debar, Mephibosheth was returning to the palace.

The young man was so crippled that someone had to go get him. He was brought by the king from one side of courageous to the other. He now lived in the palace and ate at the king's table. Not only Mephibosheth, but his entire household as well, was blessed in this way. "And Mephibosheth lived in

Jerusalem, because he always ate at the king's table, and he was crippled in both feet" (2 Sam. 9:13).

The great news is that no one can tell who is crippled when you are all sitting and eating at the king's table. Wow! Mephibosheth's story sounds like mine and the story of many others. Crippled by a fall, sought by a king, found in a far country, and saved for another's sake, we have finally been restored to the king's table!

The King has not forgotten about you. He is seeking you out. He will rescue you from a dry and barren place and bring you back to the right side of courageous. God is a restorer! I am living proof of that. What He has done for me, He will do for you. He will not only restore you, but He will also restore your hopes and dreams. He will use what the devil intended for bad and make it good. He is not through with you. You are valuable to Him. After all, you are a king's kid!

Sir, ma'am, your table is ready!

Questions for Discussion:

1. Have you had a circumstance in your life that made you feel separated and isolated? What did you do to get reconnected?
2. Discuss the hopelessness Mephibosheth must have felt.
3. When others came to get him, why do you think Mephibosheth referred to himself as "a dead dog"? Do you, too, have self-esteem issues?

4. Are there any areas of your life in which you feel crippled mentally, emotionally, or spiritually? If so, what are they?
5. How does the transition to the king's table change the way a person is viewed?

NAVIGATING THROUGH YOUR STORM

*W*ednesday, September 16, 2009, was a normal day in my life as a traveling minister. I had coffee with a pastor friend of mine, lunch with some other friends, and was looking forward to church that night. I was closing a week of spiritual emphasis with my dear friends Kevin and Tami Ward, lead pastors at Central Assembly of God in Enid, Oklahoma.

Kevin and his great team were going over the evening service and had asked me to be involved in that. I had just left the planning meeting at the church and was leaving to go back to my hotel when I received a phone call that would forever change my family. The voice on the other end of the line said, "Lynn, Freda has been killed in a car accident."

A chill went through me. It was hard to believe, like I was dreaming. Then I had a sudden urgency to get to my wife, Dianna. You see, Freda was her mom and my mother-in-law.

Pastor Kevin and Tami helped me get my things packed and drove me to Oklahoma City. My brother, Dennis, met me there and drove me to where the rest of the family was. The accident had happened in Arkansas about an hour and a half from our house. During this time, I wanted to call my wife, but she was home alone and I did not want to tell her when she was by herself. I called our pastors, Randy and Patty Long, and they were soon on their way. Finally, Patty and some of Dianna's friends made it to our house and informed her of the accident. Obviously, she was devastated. We quickly made plans to meet at a church in the town where the accident had happened. It seemed like it took forever for me to get to Dianna.

Let me push the rewind button for a moment. The reason my in-laws had been visiting at our house was that my wife was having some medical tests run. I had to be out of town, so Ken and Freda had gone over to our house so that Freda could go with Dianna to her doctor's appointment. At that time Ken and Freda were the pastors at Faith Temple in Bixby, Oklahoma, so they were trying to get back for their Wednesday evening service when the accident happened.

Just fifteen minutes after my wife was told that her mother had passed away, she received a call from the doctor's office. They had found a mass in her stomach. Needless to say, the storm was raging around us and our entire family. We were confused and numbed by the news. We were definitely on the other side of courageous right now. Dianna and I opted to stay involved with the rest of the family as far as preparing for the funeral. But that was nothing new. My wife is always putting others first.

I wish I could say to you that if you are a follower of Jesus Christ, nothing bad will ever happen to you, that you will never experience a storm or a heartache. That is not only not true, but it is also not scriptural. The Bible is very clear that we are not exempt from the storms of life. "In this world you will have trouble," says John 16:33. "Be patient in affliction," Paul wrote in Romans 12:12. Why would he write that if we were not going to experience affliction?

The apostle Paul was shipwrecked, beaten, and imprisoned. Stephen was stoned to death. John was marooned on the island of Patmos and left to die. These are just a few examples of what great men of God went through. They all experienced times of difficulty and distress, times of pain and confusion.

As someone who has lived through several storms of life, I can tell you that God is still a faithful God. He is a very present help in time of trouble. He has never left me or forsaken me. Let me say it clearly: being a Christian does not remove you from the world and its problems, but rather it equips you to live productively and victoriously in spite of what you go through.

I have had to stand many times on Deuteronomy 29:29: "The secret things belong to God, but the things that are revealed belong to us." I am fully convinced there are some things we will never understand until we get to heaven. The secret things belong to God. I am not trying to understand God; I am only trying to trust Him, even in the middle of a storm. Most assuredly, you can trust Him. Do not look at God through your storm, but look at your storm through God! As Psalm 31:23 reminds us, "The Lord preserves the faithful"; and Psalm 31:24 says, "Be strong and take heart all you who hope in the Lord."

Let's take a look at a couple of different storms in Scripture and see what we can learn from them. The first storm I want to look at is found in Matthew 8:23–27:

> Then he got in to the boat and his disciples followed him. Without warning, a furious storm came up on the lake, so that the waves swept over the boat. But Jesus was sleeping. The disciples went and woke him, saying, "Lord, save us! We are going to drown!"
>
> He replied, "You of little faith, why are so afraid?" Then he got up and rebuked the winds and the waves, and it was completely calm.
>
> The men were amazed and asked, "What kind of man is this? Even the winds and waves obey him!"

From this passage of Scripture, I have learned several things about the storms of life:

1. Following Jesus means you will face storms in your life.

   Verse 23 says, "His disciples followed him." These men were following wherever Jesus led them, and that included going through a storm.

2. Our reaction to storms is very different from Jesus' reaction.

We panic! The disciples cried out, "We are going to drown!" Jesus, however, had a different reaction. Notice also that Jesus addressed His disciples' lack of faith and their fear before He rebuked the storm on their behalf: "You of little faith, why are you so afraid?" (v. 26).

3. Storms are no respecter of persons.

Jesus Himself faced storms. Storms are not going to skip by the rich and famous. *Everyone* experiences them.

4. Storms have a way of making you think your temporary situation is permanent.

After Jesus rebuked the winds and the waves, "it was completely calm," as verse 26 says. When you are in a storm, the enemy may tell you that it will always be this way and that your life will be nothing but a constant storm, but the devil is a liar! As long as Jesus is in your life, "completely calm" can manifest. I speak "completely calm" over you today!

5. Storms give us new revelation of Jesus.

After the storm was over, the disciples asked, "What kind of man is this? Even the winds and waves obey him!" I pray that once your storm is calmed, you will have a new revelation of Jesus that you did not have before. He will show Himself to you in the storm, so stay faithful.

The other storm I want to take a look at is found in Acts 27:13–15. This is the same storm I referred to in the chapter on my divorce. I want to look at it in greater depth in this chapter.

The passage reads: "When a gentle south wind began to blow, they thought they had obtained what they wanted; so they weighed anchor and sailed along the shore of Crete. Before very long, a wind of hurricane force, called a northeaster, swept down from the island. The ship was caught by the storm and could not head in to the wind; so we gave way to it and were driven along."

Let's stop right here for a moment. This storm, like the storm in Matthew, reveals some important things. As we read through the rest of this chapter in Acts, we will notice some key principles that will help us while we are navigating the storms of life. I trust the following principles will help you as they have helped me so many times in my life.

6. In a storm, it takes all our energy to hold it all together.

   "When the men had hoisted it aboard, they passed ropes under the ship itself to hold it together" (v. 17).

In the middle of my storm, it was all I could do to hold it together. Sometimes it feels like that is all we can do—hold it together, survive. It is a very exhausting process. It is mentally, physically, emotionally, and even spiritually exhausting. When the storm is intense, do your part to hold it together. God has promised to do the rest.

7. Storms reveal our priorities.

"We took such a violent battering from the storm that the next day they began to throw the cargo overboard" (v. 18).

The men aboard the ship realized the severity of the storm was causing them to sink, so they got rid of the cargo. When we are going through a storm, some things have to be thrown overboard for us to survive. If you are in the middle of a storm right now, ask God if there is any spiritual baggage that you need to throw overboard. Are there any habits, addictions, or even people in your life that might need to be removed? For me, the answer was an emphatic yes.

8 Storms cause hope to waver.

"When neither sun nor stars appeared for many days and the storm continued raging, we finally gave up all hope of being saved" (v. 20).

In Psalm 42:5 and Psalm 42:11, the psalmist faced such a fierce storm that he started talking to himself in an effort to bolster his faith. In both verses he asked, "Why are you downcast, O my soul?" However, he knew that though tears had been his food both day and night, and the storm was raging all around, he had hope. In both verses, he reminded himself to put his hope in God.

I would remind you of that today as well. Do not give up. As long as you have Him, you have hope!

9. Storms reveal our bad decisions.

"After the men had gone a long time without food, Paul stood up before them and said, 'Men, you should have taken my advice not to sail from Crete; then you would have spared yourself this damage and loss' " (v. 21).

Paul wanted the men to know that they were in this situation because of a bad decision. The storm had revealed that. Every one of us knows what it is to make a bad decision. Sometimes we realize that we have made a poor decision without going through a storm, but there are other times when it takes a storm for us to know that. My personal experience has been that a storm often magnifies bad decisions.

Since decisions determine our destination, they cannot be taken lightly. I always give two warnings to people who have tough decisions to make:

1. Never make a decision without praying about it. It is very important to get God involved in every decision you make. He is the Lord of your life. Give Him a chance to speak to you.
2. Never make a decision when you are under a great deal of stress. I know a lot of you just laughed out loud. You may be saying, "Lynn, I am always under stress. If I go by that rule, then I will never be able to make a decision in my life." If that is the case, may I refer you back to what I just said above—pray! Do not skip it. It is vital to your good decision-making process. (Please look back at the chapter "Get on Your knees and Fight Like a Man.")

10. Storms remind us of the Lord's presence.

   "Last night an angel of God whose I am and whom I serve stood beside me and said, 'Do not be afraid, Paul. You must stand trial before Caesar; and God has graciously given you the lives of all who sail with you' " (v. 23).

   Paul rose to encourage his shipmates, even in the middle of a storm. When we are helpless and it looks hopeless, the Lord is still with us. He never leaves us or forsakes us—not even in a storm.

In Psalm 23:4, David said it this way: "Even though I walk through the valley of the shadow of death, I will fear no evil, for you are with me." Even in the valley, David acknowledged the Lord's presence.

I have no idea the magnitude of the storm in your life, but I do know what I have been through. I know that storms are intense. I know that I thought I was a goner when I faced my storm. But I also know this: the Lord was with me! Take comfort in that today. Right now you are just trying to hold yourself and everything else together, but always acknowledge Him, even in the storm. Talk to Him, and let Him love on you. He wants to.

11. Storms drive us to unfamiliar territory.

"When daylight came, they did not recognize the land, but they saw a bay with a sandy beach, where they decided to run the ship aground if they could" (v. 39).

Friends, please notice the line in that verse that says "they did not recognize the land." The storm had taken them to an unfamiliar place, a place they did not know and a place they never thought they would be. In our storms, we, too, do not know where we are or why we are there.

I certainly never dreamed I would go through a divorce. But I did. The storm of that drove me to a place I never thought I would be. I did not

95

know what to do or how to act. I'm sure you can relate. You have been through things you thought you would never go through in life. It has taken you to unfamiliar places. It is frightening and confusing. The only thing both you and I can rest in is the presence of the Lord. He is still the God of unfamiliar territory.

God even gives us favor in the unfamiliar. When the men arrived on that island called Malta (Acts 28:1), Scripture says that "the islanders showed us unusual kindness" (v. 2). God was not only present with them, but He was showing favor in the unfamiliar territory!

12. Miracles happen in spite of the storm.

Paul gathered a pile of brushwood and, as he put it on the fire, a viper, driven out by the heat, fastened itself on his hand. When the islanders saw the snake hanging from his hand, they said to each other, "This man must be a murderer; for though he escaped from the sea, justice has not allowed him to live." But Paul shook the snake off in the fire and suffered no ill effects. The people expected him to swell up or suddenly fall dead, but after waiting a long time and seeing nothing unusual happen to him, they changed their minds and said he was a god.

There was an estate nearby that belonged to Publius, the chief official of the island. He welcomed us to his home and for three days entertained us hospitably. His father was sick in bed, suffering from fever and dysentery. Paul went in to see him, and after prayer, placed his hands on him and healed him. When this happened, the rest of the sick on the island came and were cured. They honored us in so many ways and when we were ready to sail, they furnished us with the supplies we needed.

—ACTS 28:3–10

These are powerful verses. Paul and the other men were not headed to Malta, and when they got there, they were in unfamiliar territory. They were there only because a strong storm that was out of their control had pushed them there. However, in spite of the unplanned visit, God's miracle-working power showed up, and many people were healed. Something powerful and positive came out of their unplanned visit. God's power was greater than the power of the storm!

It is the same for you. You may be facing something that you never planned for, and you may be there only because a storm pushed you in that direction. But God will show Himself mighty and powerful in spite of the storm. You cannot see it now, but your miracle is coming. The storm changed your direction, but not your God. He is still a miracle worker.

Oh yeah, I forgot to finish the story about Dianna's bad news from her doctor's visit. About a month after her mom's funeral, we finally got to go back for more tests. Anytime you hear the word *mass* from the medical professionals, it is not good.

We arrived at the doctor's office and nervously waited. When they called Dianna to the back, I went with her. They laid her on the table, and I took a seat in the corner of the room. They had already put up a copy of Dianna's last X-ray, and I could see the mass very clearly. I prayed quietly in the corner of the room.

I was positioned so that I could easily see the monitor, and I watched as the nurse took a wand-like device and began to move it over my wife's stomach. The image showed up immediately. I am not a medical professional, but I did notice there was nothing unusual on the screen. The nurse looked confused. She put down the device, walked over to the first X-ray, and looked at it intently. She came back and tried again to find the mass, but again, there was nothing! She asked Dianna, "What are you in for?" and Dianna informed her that she had come in because they had found a mass in her stomach. The nurse said, "I see it on the X-ray, but it is not there now. Let me take a picture to show the doctor. I will be back." We waited maybe two minutes, and then the nurse returned. "You can leave now. Whatever it was, it is gone now!"

Many will give their own thoughts on the dramatic turnaround, but Dianna and I know in our hearts that God took the mass away. That was God showing Himself as a miracle worker in the middle of our family storm. Keep navigating through your storm. God is with you every step of the way!

For many of you, a storm has blown you to the other side of courageous. The Lord once gave me a verse in the middle of one of my storms. It is a verse that I hold on to every time I go through a storm, and I pray it will help you too. It is found in Proverbs 10:25 and says, "When the storm has swept by, the wicked are gone, but the righteous stand firm forever."

Stand firm, my friend!

Questions for Discussion:

1. Has a storm ever devastated your life? Did it catch you off guard? Share what happened.
2. As a Christ-follower, what steps should you take in navigating through the storms of life?
3. What has been your reaction when those close to you experience storms? Would you do anything different next time?
4. Discuss the difference in our reaction to storms as compared to Jesus' reaction regarding storms.
5. Have you ever made a major decision in the middle of a storm? Why is that not a good idea?

Instrument Rated

*T*here are hundreds of thousands of pilots who have learned to fly a small aircraft. They have the ability to take off, maneuver safely, and land the plane without incident. However, they can do this successfully only if they can see where they are going. Once they have the plane in the air, they must find landmarks by which to fly. It might be rivers, lakes, highways, mountain ranges, or something else. Regardless of the specific landmark, pilots use them to guide them toward their desired destination.

The problem arises when pilots are socked by a storm. If a storm obstructs their line of vision and they can no longer locate their landmarks, confusion and panic can quickly set it. They were relying on their sight to get them to their destination, but now they cannot see. Soon vertigo or disorientation may set in. Vertigo is a sensation of dizziness in which an individual feels that either he or his surroundings are whirling. In other words, when these pilots can no longer see, they lose their sense of direction.

You may remember the story of the death of John F. Kennedy, Jr. On Friday, July 16, 1999, he and two passengers left a New York City airport bound for Martha's Vineyard to attend a family wedding-rehearsal dinner. Another pilot, Kyle Bailey, was planning on making the same trip that evening, but because of the weather, he opted out. John Jr. decided to fly anyway.

According to the National Transportation Board, John Jr. received a private- pilot certificate in April 1998. He had three hundred hours of total flight experience, but he had no instrument rating. He and his passengers died that night as their plane collided with the water at full speed. The storm had socked him in, and because he was not instrument rated and lost sight of his landmarks, he collided with the water. Many believe that vertigo set in and that John had no idea he was headed toward the water. He thought he was flying along on a normal route, but in reality, he was disoriented and confused by a storm that ultimately took his life.

Then there are other pilots who do not fly according to what they see, but according to the instruments in front of them. They do not have to trust landmarks to guide them; that is what their instruments do. These pilots have received an instrument rating. In order to achieve this, they have to spend hours of training in simulated storm conditions. They don't just crawl into the cockpit of a plane and deem themselves "instrument rated." No, they have to put in the time to learn to respond, not according to what they see, but according to what the instruments say.

They are trained to totally and completely trust and depend on the instruments.

It is the same way in following Christ. I know many Christ-followers who do really well as long as their lives are going smoothly. However, if they ever experience a storm, spiritual vertigo sets in and they become spiritually disoriented. The hardship they experience literally causes them to lose their sense of direction. They know that God has them on a path and is taking them somewhere, but they can no longer see clearly. Their spiritual sight has been blocked by the storm.

Then there are other believers who do not go through life living according to what they can see, but trusting the one they cannot see. They have put much time into prayer and reading the Word of God. They know Jesus—not just *about* Jesus, but they *know* Jesus! Their intimate relationship with the Lord brings them to a level of trusting Him and His Word above all else, including their own thoughts or feelings. It takes time and discipline to get to this point, but it is possible.

When privately licensed pilots take off, they must be prepared to turn away from any confrontation with a storm. This may require getting off course perhaps several times in order to make it to their destination. They must respect the storm because it can put them and any passengers in immediate danger. However, if the pilots are instrument rated, they fix their eyes on the instrument panel in front of them, knowing the instruments will guide them through the storm.

They trust that the instruments will not fail them. The hours of training and preparation now pay off.

I want to discipline myself to keep my eyes on the instruments (God and His Word) when I am going through a storm. Fellow believer, I know that being an instrument-rated Christian will give us confidence to move forward on the path the Lord has set for us and help us to realize that every attack from the enemy will be in vain. In fact, the enemy does not have a storm strong enough to cause us to crash!

You may be thinking that things are good for you right now and that this does not apply to you. Friend, I believe God expects us to prepare for the storm before it arrives, not just pray for help after it gets here. I believe God expects us to do our part.

It is like a student who knows a test is coming, but just prays for help rather than studying. Oh, that student may walk into the class for the test and find the teacher gone and the answers lying open on the desk. He might even excitedly claim Jeremiah 33:3: "Call to me and I will answer you and tell you great and unsearchable things you do not know." However, that isn't God. He won't help you cheat, so prepare!

There are three reasons I am asking you to prepare even before you feel like you are on the other side of courageous:

1. I do not want a storm to cause you to crash. It doesn't have to. It may get dark and bumpy, but you will not crash!

2. I do not want you to lose your sense of direction. Stay on the path the Lord has placed you on by staying focused on His Word.
3. I do not want you to miss your promotion. Every time a student passes the big test, he is promoted to the next grade. Pass the test the enemy has brought your way, and get your promotion. God will use you like never before!

I grew up in the town of Moore, Oklahoma, a suburb on the south side of Oklahoma City. When I was high school age, there was only one high school, but now there are three. The city of Moore is a rapidly growing area between Oklahoma City and Norman, home of the Oklahoma Sooners (Do you like the way I slid that in?)

When I was in high school, my aunt and uncle, Cecil and Gwen Wheeler, owned a Tastee Freeze. In case you have never heard of those, they are much like Dairy Queens. They used to be very popular in our area and served great ice cream and burgers. What else do you need as a teenager?

I will never forget one afternoon when we received a phone call from Uncle Cecil that the Tastee Freeze had caught on fire. My dad had just gotten home from work when the call came. He rushed my mom, my brother, and me to the car and drove quickly toward the restaurant. It was not a far drive, so after only one turn, we could see the smoke rising in the air. We arrived to the sight of firefighters frantically working to put out the fire. My aunt, uncle, cousins, and quite a few local people had gathered in the parking lot. My family and I got out of the car and joined them.

I was in eleventh grade at the time and had never known anyone who had experienced a fire, much less close relatives. We got out of the car to try to find out what had happened and whether the business could be saved. My family quickly got caught up in the crowd, and as a teenager, I was mesmerized by all that was going on.

Obviously, there was a lot of hugging, comforting, and praying taking place. A great deal of movement and shifting was also occurring, and both conversation and crying abounded. It was a very emotional time for all of us. With all of the constant movement, I eventually found myself standing next to Aunt Gwen. We stood there for a few moments with our arms around each other, talking about what had happened. After a few minutes, my aunt looked at me and said, "Well, Lynn, all things do work together for good to those that love God and are called according to His purposes." She was referencing a great scripture that Paul gave to the church at Rome. In the New International Version, it reads like this: "And we know that in all things God works for the good of those who love him, who have been called according to his purpose."

I mean no disrespect at all, but I will admit that my first thought was, *Aunt Gwen, you are a nut!* I wondered if she realized that her business was burning, that her source of income had just disappeared. She should have been filled with questions, I thought, but yet she was quoting Scripture and trusting God.

As I reflect on that story, I realize that Aunt Gwen and I were on two different spiritual levels. She was "instrument rated," and I was not. Like Job, she knew that her possessions were not her entire life. She understood fully that according to her instruments (God and the Bible), God would meet all her needs and take care of her through every storm of life. She was fully focused on God and His Word and not the circumstances that surrounded her.

It was not much of a lesson to me then as a teenaged boy, but now it is forever embedded in my mind. Aunt Gwen's faith in God in the middle of a storm speaks volumes to me today. Her eyes were not on the storm, but on the Man who speaks to the storm and the storm obeys!

I have a good friend, Nick, who is a pilot for American Airlines. Nick and I met a few years ago in a church where I am a frequent ministry guest. A few years ago when I came to his church and preached about being instrument-rated Christians, he gave me some good thoughts to add to my message. Since then, we talk about this analogy every time we get together. Even though I am not a pilot, I love talking about this example. As a frequent flyer, it has really opened my eyes too.

Nick recently shared with me about one of the key instruments in the cockpit of the plane. It is called an attitude indicator. Nick said, "The attitude indicator is the central or main instrument. Instrument flying uses the hub-and-spoke concept, like a bicycle wheel, with the attitude indicator in the middle." I was blown away by his words and how they relate to us on the other side of courageous. Our attitude is crucial; it is the center of it all. Wow!

Nick went on to say, "Pilots reference other instruments, but *always* come back to the attitude indicator. They can be in thick fog or heavy storm clouds yet know that they are flying straight and level. So the attitude indicator is like the Word of God. We can reference other things, but we must always come back to that."

I was absorbing every word Nick was saying and thinking, *That will preach!* But Nick's following words brought conviction to me. "On an airliner," he said, "there are three attitude indicators. Each pilot has one, plus there is a backup. They are independent of each other, as they each have their own power source and gyro."

In the middle of a storm, our attitude indicator is so important. We each have one. How is yours? I confess, I sure need help from the Lord at times with mine, so I try to remember that a good attitude will help me get back to the right side of courageous. Remember, our attitude determines our altitude! We can soar high with Christ, even during our storms, if we keep a right attitude. It is part of our instrument rating.

The year 1999 was a difficult one for me. It seemed like one storm after another came across my path. Have you ever been there? Well, that's where I was. It seemed like I got through one thing only to face another thing, and so on and so on. I was definitely on the other side of courageous. The only way

I made it through was with the help of my instruments (God and His Word) and my friends.

One of those friends is a guy by the name of Pat Schaztline. Pat and I met many years ago when I was speaking at an Indiana youth camp. Pat has an incredible traveling ministry, and to this day he continues to invest in the lives of students in this generation.

On February 23, 1999, Pat took a moment out of his busy schedule to write me a letter. I have carried it with me for all these years. In fact, I never leave town to speak at any ministry event without this letter going with me. It serves as a reminder to me of the friends who stood with me in my time of trial and of the fact that God is *always* faithful. This letter had such an impact on my life that, with Pat's permission, I have decided to share it with you. Here is the letter I received from a friend when I was on the other side of courageous and trying to make it back:

Dear Lynn,

I have been praying for you daily! I believe that God has anointed you to preach His Word to the nations. Only in the last two years have I come to understand the intense drain of evangelism. The rewards are awesome, but the enemy attacks us with great fury. Stand firm, my friend, and please know that we love you. Thank you for being a mentor for years.

Last year, in a hotel, God changed me. My son was sick, and I could not get home. For seven hours, I wrestled until He called me by name out of my tomb. You have changed so many lives, Lynn. I want to stand behind you when we get to heaven and see thousands line up to say thank you to Lynn Wheeler.

People do not realize that it is expensive to be effective. Many times the development of God's picture takes place in the darkroom. But it is not over! When you have done all that you can do, just stand. While others are abandoning you, God is commanding His charge over you.

Please call if you need us.

Sincerely,

Pat Schatzline
Mercy Seat Ministries, Inc.

I still tear up every time I read that letter. It was God inspired for me at that moment in my life, and it still speaks volumes to me today.

That letter may speak to you also. I know that where you are may not be where you want to be. But know that God is taking charge! Take it from a guy who has been on the other side of courageous but was brought back by the power of God. He has a reputation for doing that. Just change the names in that letter and let it encourage you today.

Questions for Discussion:

1. From a spiritual perspective, what does the term *instrument rating* mean to you?
2. Why do we have a tendency to take our eyes off the instruments and look at the storm? Why is this spiritually dangerous?
3. Who in the Bible comes to your mind when we talk about taking our eyes off the instruments? What was the end result for them?
4. Have you ever taken your eyes off the instruments during a spiritual storm? What did you learn from that?
5. What are some action steps we can take to discipline ourselves to stay focused on God's Word regardless of what is going on around us?

From Battle to Blessing

*H*ow many times have you heard someone in church leadership or someone leading a worship experience say something like, "You are a *blessed* child of God"? Immediately you think they are not talking to you, because you do not feel blessed at all.

I know that some of you reading this right now do not feel favored or blessed by God. In fact, many of you feel as though your entire life has been nothing but one battle after another. As you are reading this right now, you feel so weary from the battle. It has you mentally, physically, emotionally, and spiritually exhausted.

I want to stop right now and give you some very powerful words from Jesus that I have had to lean on many times. Jesus says to us in Matthew 11:28–30, "Come to me, all you who are weary and burdened, and I will give you rest. Take my yoke upon you and learn from me, for I am gentle and humble in heart, and you will find rest for your souls. For my yoke is easy and my burden light."

I know that for some of you, it seems like the battles never end. You just move from one to another. You have a physical battle, and you get through that . . . then there is a family battle, and you get through that . . . then there is a financial battle, and you get through that . . . and on and on it goes. Your life has been a consistent and constant cycle of one battle after another, and you do not feel blessed and favored in the least. No, you feel more like a battle-weary believer who hopes he can hang on to the end.

Well, I have a word for you from the Word of God! Second Chronicles 20:15 says, "Listen, King Jehoshaphat and all who live in Judah and Jerusalem! This is what the Lord says to you: 'Do not be afraid or discouraged because of this vast army. For the battle is not yours, but God's.'" Friend, please focus on these words here: *"The battle is not yours, but God's."* Give the battle to Him—it is not yours!

Verse 17 goes on to say, "You will not have to fight this battle. Take up your positions: stand firm and see the deliverance the Lord will give you, O Judah and Jerusalem. Do not be afraid; do not be discouraged. Go out to face them tomorrow, and the Lord will be with you." Stand firm in your faith, my friend, and watch the Lord's hand work for you. Watch Him move you from the battle to the blessings!

Let's take a minute and talk about blessings. The reason I want to do this is that so many people really believe that all that word means is "money." They think that when we say someone is blessed, we really mean they are financially prosperous. I want to move you out of that mind-set. I want to show you that being blessed is so much more than being financially prosperous.

Here are three things I want you to know about blessings:

1. BLESSINGS BRING JOY AND NOT SORROW.

   Proverbs 10:22 says, "The blessing of the Lord makes rich and adds no sorrow." You see, you are not blessed because you are rich, but you are rich because you are blessed. You are not blessed because you are healed, but you are healed because you are blessed. You are a blessed child of God. The Bible says you are, so you are! Regardless of the battle going on around you, God's blessings will bring joy and not sorrow.

2. BLESSINGS ARE OFTEN MISUNDERSTOOD.

   As a child, I grew up in church. I heard the words *blessed* and *blessings* many times. I watched people cry at an altar and listened as someone told me those people were being blessed. I could go on and on with similar examples that demonstrate that many people really believe that being blessed by God has to do with some outward display of emotion. While that may be a part of it, it is so much more than that, my friend.

Being blessed is more than an outward display of emotion, and it is more than being financially prosperous. I know people who would say to me, "Lynn, if I could just have one day of peace in my home, I would feel blessed." Others would say, " Lynn, if I could wake up one day and go all day without pain in my body, I would feel blessed."

Do not misunderstand me. I want you all to be financially blessed. I hope you get a million dollars in the mail tomorrow! However, I also want to make clear that blessing is about so much more than just money. You see, I want you to live without pain in your body, and I want you to have peace in your home, too. I want you to have a strong marriage. I want you to have whatever you need in this life to live the blessed life God wants to give you.

My prayer is that you will move out of every battle and into the realm of *every* blessing that the Lord has for you.

3. BLESSINGS COME TO THOSE WHO FEAR THE LORD.

Let's examine Psalm 112:1–8 for a moment. Verse 1 of this psalm supports my third point as it says, "Blessed is the man who fears the Lord, who finds great delight in his commands." From that verse, we can see that blessings come to those who fear the Lord.

Awesome! However, you might be wondering what kind of blessings the psalmist is talking about. The next seven verses answer that question.

Verse 2: "His children will be mighty in the land; the generation of the upright will be blessed." Yes! Our children will be mighty in the land. If we fear the Lord, this is one of the blessings that will come to pass, according to Scripture. Call your children by name right now and declare them to be mighty in the land!

I know some of you reading this have children who do not serve the Lord. I pray the Lord would bring them into right relationship with Him. Never give up praying for them. Claim them for God, and stand on His promise.

Verse 3: "Wealth and riches are in his house, and his righteousness endures forever." Wow! I receive that one too! May I continue to obey God's Word in the area of giving so that His promises will be released in my direction. Do you receive that?

Verse 4: "Even in darkness light dawns for the upright, for the gracious and compassionate and righteous man." Even in our darkest hour, God is still faithful. The light will dawn on those who fear the Lord.

Verse 5: "Good will come to him who is generous and lends freely, who conducts his affairs with justice." Simply put, if we are generous and lend freely, and conduct our affairs with justice, we will be blessed.

Verses 6–7: "Surely he will never be shaken; a righteous man will be remembered forever. He will have no fear of bad news; his heart is steadfast trusting in the Lord." The battle may get you down, but you will never be out. Trust in the Lord!

Verse 8: "His heart is secure, he will have no fear; in the end he will look in triumph on his foes." Sometimes in the middle of the battle, it does not appear that we are victorious or even have a chance of victory. However, this verse reminds us that in the end, *we win!*

At the time of the writing of this book, I have a friend who is in a battle for his marriage. Right now it does not look like he is going to win that battle. It appears that despite his best efforts, divorce will happen. He has prayed and fought for his marriage for many months. However, it takes two people to be married.

Some of you have been there in your marriage or in other areas of your life. Please know that the outcome of the battle does not determine your blessings from God. He loves you! And even when one battle seems to be over, remember, it is not the end of the battle, only the end of that particular one. As long as we live, we will have battles, but the Lord is mighty in every one. Psalm 24:8 says, "Who is this King of glory? The Lord strong and mighty, the Lord mighty in battle."

God's favor wants to move into your life to move you from the *battle* to the *blessings*. The Lord is mighty in battle, and you are blessed!

If you find yourself in a spiritual battle today, let me give you some principles that I hope will sustain you and lead you to victory:

1. PUT ON THE FULL ARMOR OF GOD (Eph. 6:1–8).

Don't just put on part of the armor. Victory will require all parts.

2. DO NOT LISTEN TO THE ENEMY.

Can the enemy really speak to us? If he spoke to Jesus in Matthew 4, he will surely try to deceive us with his words as well. Be on guard against Satan's three biggest lies:

a. No hope—Satan will try to tell you that your current situation will always be this way, that it will never improve or go away. But the devil is a liar! Jesus said of him in John 8:44, "When he lies, he speaks his native language, for he is a liar and the father of lies."

b. No harm—He wants you to think that the way you are living and the things you are doing are not harming anyone. Therefore, he says, it is all right, and the secret sin is really okay. Again, the devil is a liar! "Do not be deceived; God cannot be mocked. A man reaps what he sows" (Gal. 6:7).

c. No hurry—The enemy wants you to think there is no hurry. Keep doing what you are doing and living like you are living, he says. Life on the other side of courageous is not that bad. Take your time and live it up, because you will have time to make it right with the Lord. Once more, the devil is a liar! Procrastination is the devil's workshop.

You see, whenever the enemy opens his mouth, he is lying. You cannot listen to him, especially in the middle of a spiritual battle when you are weak and vulnerable. Listening to the enemy did not work out so well for Eve in the Garden of Eden (Gen. 3:1–2). Remember, there is no need to even start a conversation with someone who wants to destroy you—and that is exactly what the devil wants to do!

3. RELY ON THE WEAPON OF WEAKNESS.

Believe it or not, weakness is a weapon. It is a weapon because it magnifies God's strength in us. When we are weak, He is strong. I love the words of Paul in 2 Corinthians 12:9: "But he said to me, 'My grace is sufficient for you, for my power is made perfect in weakness.' Therefore I will boast all the more gladly about my weaknesses, so that Christ's power may rest on me."

Here are some tips for using your weaknesses as weapons:

a. Recognize and acknowledge the presence of weakness.
b. Realize the purpose for it. God may not remove it.
c. Review what your weaknesses reveal about you. Never stop working on the weak areas of your life. We all have them, but with God's help, we can overcome.
d. Resist responding in the wrong way. Don't ignore, excuse, deny, or defend your weaknesses. Be honest and accountable; it will help you even in battle. I have learned if I accept respon-

sibility for my shortcomings, receive forgiveness from God and others, and then move on, I am somehow stronger in the Lord for battle against the enemy.

e. Remember the promise of God. Even when you are in the most intense battle, His grace is sufficient. You can make it through the battle—that is God's promise to you.

f. Rely on God's power. Your weakness plus God's power will equal victory for you. Weakness really is a weapon!

4. CONTINUALLY DRAW STRENGTH FROM THE LORD.

God is our source of strength. Others may encourage us, but He sustains us. I know you get weary in the battle at times. Earlier in this chapter, I said that sometimes it seems like the battle will never end, and that in itself makes us even wearier. Here are a few power verses on strength to remind us where our strength comes from:

"The Lord is my strength and my song" (Ex. 15:2).

"It is God who arms me with strength and makes my way perfect" (2 Sam. 22:33).

"The Lord is my strength and my shield; my heart trusts in him and I am helped" (Ps. 28:7).

"I can do everything through him who gives me strength" (Phil. 4:13).

"The name of the Lord is a strong tower" (Prov. 18:10).

"Be strong in the Lord and in his mighty power" (Eph. 6:10).

5. KEEP INVESTING IN OTHERS.

Sometimes when we are in the heat of battle, we tend to develop an inward focus. We get so caught up in our lives and what is going on with us that we lose focus of others. I know firsthand that when you are on the other side of courageous, you go into survival mode, just trying to keep your head above water. But I also know that it is important, even in the middle of battle, to keep serving, keep ministering, and keep reaching out to those in need.

This is a principle I wish I had discovered early in my life and ministry. Unfortunately, I did not really grasp this until about fifteen years ago. However, once I understood the importance of investing in others (not just financially), it brought a powerful momentum to my life. That is why I recommend it to you.

"You will always have everything you want in life if you will help enough people get what they want," says Zig Ziglar. And as Proverbs 11:25 reminds us, "He who refreshes others will himself be refreshed." I think both those thoughts can be summed up in some words I recently saw on a poster: "You cannot hold a light to brighten another's path without also brightening your own."

Friend, stay faithful in the battle. The Lord has promised His help. Rest assured, He will help you get back to courageous!

Questions for Discussion:

1. Talk about the most intense battle you have ever personally been through. What were its lasting effects on your life?
2. Review Ephesians 6:1–8. Why is *every* piece of the armor of God important?
3. We have learned that the battle is the Lord's, so why do we struggle so much with giving our problems to Him?
4. Are you helping someone through a battle right now? Is it affecting you in any way? Share your thoughts.
5. Whom have you blessed lately? Have you spoken blessings over your wife or children today?

SEASONS OF NOTHING

*H*ow many of you are currently praying about something, but God has not yet answered your prayer? Come on, raise your hand. Well, if you did not raise your hand, then please write a book or do a seminar to show the rest of us how to get *all* our prayers answered. In reality, we all have some things we have been praying about that we are waiting on the Lord to respond to.

On the other side of courageous, I often found myself crying out to God but getting no response. I found myself reaching for Him but not feeling a thing. I call times like that "seasons of nothing." We have all been there, and perhaps some of you are there even now.

Seasons of nothing are challenging because we know God answers prayer— after all, He has done it for us before—but now He seems silent. When we face such times, we can take encouragement from these words from the apostle Paul: "Therefore we do not lose heart. Though outwardly we are wasting away, yet inwardly we are being renewed day by day.

123

For our light and momentary troubles are achieving for us an eternal glory that far outweighs them all. So we fix our eyes not on what is seen, but on what is unseen. For what is seen is temporary, but what is unseen is eternal" (2 Cor. 4:16–18).

Repeat this after me: "What I see . . . is not all there is!" Please say it again: "What I see . . . is not all there is!" Repeat it until you get it. Paul is reminding us not to focus on what we see, but on what we cannot see. That is where the value is, and that is what is eternal. That is what will sustain us on the other side of courageous. Knowing that there is more going on than what I can see actually keeps me moving some days. If what I see was all I had . . . whew, thank God there is more! I want to be faithful in seasons of nothing.

Before we go any further, let's take a look at the word *nothing*. I submit to you that the word is over-used in the English language, and when we use it, we often don't really mean "nothing." For example, I often tease my wife (ladies, you may be guilty too) when she looks into a closet full of clothes and says she has "nothing" to wear. Seriously? My kids will open the fridge, which is full of food, but say there is "nothing" to eat. What? People sit down in front of a television with a hundred channels to choose from and declare there is "nothing" to watch? (Okay, I will give you that one!) This is one of my favorites: when kids sit around the house and say, "I'm bored. There's 'nothing' to do!" Huh? Oh yes there is! You could clean your room!

Thanks for letting me have a little fun there. Nonetheless, I've established my point. The word is overused, and most of the time when we use it, we do not really mean "nothing."

However, when we begin to talk about spiritual things, seasons of nothing are not humorous at all. In fact, they are confusing and devastating at times. When you pray and nothing changes, you can easily become very discouraged. I have seen so many people give up during seasons of nothing. Don't let that be you.

In this chapter, I want to encourage you in your season of nothing. You see, getting back to the courageous side requires faithfulness even when you cannot see God at work. It requires a faith level that says you trust Him in spite of the fact that you see nothing happening on your behalf.

Here are the three main things I encourage you to do in seasons of nothing:

1. KEEP REACHING FOR JESUS.

That's what the woman in Mark 5 did. Verses 25–26 describe her condition: "A woman was there who had been subject to bleeding for twelve years. She had suffered a great deal under the care of many doctors and had spent all she had, yet instead of getting better, she grew worse."

Now let's examine this woman's season of nothing. I'm sure most of us can relate to what she was going through.

a. Duration—This woman had already suffered for twelve years. You must admit, that is a long time!
b. Desperation—She had seen many doctors, all to no avail. In our seasons of nothing, we sometimes do everything we can think of. We are desperate for help, so we search everywhere and look for answers from everyone.
c. Irritation—It must have been very irritating for her to spend all her money on doctors who couldn't help. Now she was not only sick but also broke!
d. Frustration—This woman was in a very frustrating place, to say the least. Her season of nothing surely caused a lot of difficult emotions to surface. We can relate!

Remember, I am talking about continuing to reach for Jesus. Mark goes on to say this in verses 27–29: "When she heard about Jesus, she came up behind him in the crowd and touched His cloak, because she thought, 'If I just touch his clothes, I will be healed.' Immediately her bleeding stopped and she felt in her body that she was freed from her suffering."

I can just see a mental picture of this woman pressing through the crowd. She had been sick and bleeding for twelve years, so it stands to reason, she must have been very sick and very frail. But on this day, she had eaten her Holy Ghost Wheaties! I can just see her pushing grown men aside. Friends, she was desperate. I can see her press forward until she finally got close enough to touch Him. Then she reached out and made contact with Christ. Scripture says that *immediately* she was freed from her suffering.

This woman refused to quit reaching for Jesus, and one day she finally connected with Him. She kept reaching for Him, and when she connected, her season of nothing immediately ended. Keep reaching for Jesus! He Himself encouraged us to do just that: "Ask and it will be given you, seek and you will find, knock and the door will be opened to you" (Matt. 7:7).

2. KEEP LISTENING TO JESUS.

My supporting scripture here is one of my favorite places from which to speak. I love the story in Luke 5:1–7:

> One day as Jesus was standing by the Lake of Gennesaret, with the people crowding around Him and listening to the word of God, he saw at the water's edge two boats, left there by the fishermen who were washing their nets. He got into one of the boats, the one belonging to Simon, and asked him to push out a little from the shore. Then he sat down and taught the people from the boat.
>
> When he had finished speaking, he said to Simon, "Put out into deep water, and let down the nets for a catch."
>
> Simon answered, "Master, we have worked hard all night and haven't caught anything. But because you say so, I will let down the nets."

When they had done so, they caught such a large number of fish that their nets began to break. So they signaled their partners in the other boat to come and help them, and they came and filled both boats so full that they began to sink.

Before we proceed, there are a several things I would like to point out about Simon Peter. First of all, I have studied his personality and concluded that he was a type A person, the kind of person who has all the answers. As you read through the Gospels, you will notice that many times Jesus asked general questions directed toward everyone, but the Bible often records, "And Peter answered." Simon Peter always had the answer. Do you know people like that?

Second, I want you to understand that Peter fished as an occupation, not for sport. His fishing was not like a trip to the lake to enjoy a day of relaxation. No, Peter fished for a living. It was how he brought home the bacon, or, in this case, the fish.

Third, keep Peter's personality in mind. He often spoke before he thought.

With these things in mind, I can only imagine how Simon Peter must have felt when Jesus told him to put his nets back into the water. This was the same place where he had fished all night and caught nothing. Now he was washing his nets, his day's work finished. He was ready for a hot shower and some Kentucky-Fried chicken.

Remember, we are talking about *listening to Jesus*. Though Jesus' words went against all logic, and Peter did not feel like doing it, he obeyed the

Lord. In his season of nothing, he was still listening *and* obeying the voice of the Lord. Simon obeyed just because the Lord "said so" (v. 5).

My friend, as you walk through seasons of nothing, keep your ears tuned to heaven. Jesus still speaks to His people. Jesus said in John 10:27, "My sheep listen to my voice." Listen and obey! One word from Jesus can cancel your season of nothing and return you to courageous. One act of obedience to the words of Jesus can change everything for you. Keep listening—He is still talking to you.

3. KEEP TRUSTING IN JESUS.

One of the most incredible stories of faith in Scripture is recorded in Genesis 22:1–14. This is the story of God telling Abraham to offer his son Isaac on an altar of sacrifice. As a father, I cannot think of anything worse. Scripture very clearly says it was a test. As far as I am concerned, that would be the most grueling test of faith ever. Parents, can you relate?

God gave Abraham not only specific instructions, but also a specific region in which He was to perform the sacrifice: the region of Moriah (v. 2).

Let's look at three other things about this story:

1. Time frame—God spoke in verse 2, but Abraham did not leave until the next day (v. 3). As a parent, I can assure you that would have been a long, sleepless night. Then Abraham actually cut the wood to take with them. How do you do that, knowing what it is for?

As Abraham and Isaac journeyed to the assigned location, they had to travel for three days before they were even close enough to see it (v. 4). Time seems to drag when you are going through a test.

2. Verbalizing faith—"On the third day Abraham looked up and saw the place in the distance. He said to his servants, 'Stay here with the donkey while I and the boy go over there. We will worship and then we will come back to you' " (Gen. 22:4–5). What faith! God had told him to sacrifice his son, but in his season of nothing, Abraham spoke faith.

If I had been Abraham, I would have been frantically searching for a solution throughout the entire ordeal. Believing that it was a test and that God would not require me to sacrifice my son, I would have felt that at any time God would provide another sacrifice. I would have told myself that this was just a test to see if I would obey, and on the entire three-day journey, I would have been looking for the provision behind every tree and rock I passed. I would have been desperately searching for the animal that God would provide so that I would not have to put my boy on the altar.

But after three days—nothing! Okay, I still would have been fine because we had not yet reached the mountain. God would provide now that we had separated ourselves from our servants. It was now just my boy and I.

On that journey, Isaac noticed something. You see, Isaac had done this before. He knew the drill. He knew what a sacrifice required, and he realized that he and his father did not have the required lamb. So Isaac asked, "Father? . . . The fire and wood are here . . . but where is the lamb for the burnt offering?" (v. 7).

Abraham continued to verbalize faith in verse 8: "Abraham answered, 'God himself will provide the burnt offering for the lamb, my son.' And the two of them went on together." That was the second time Abraham spoke faith in a season of nothing. I hope you can catch that principle from God's Word.

3. Unwavering trust in God—Abraham and Isaac reached the mountain, but still there was no lamb, no provision. Abraham might have been thinking, *Maybe this isn't a test, after all. Maybe God is really asking me to put my boy on the altar. I thought He would provide, but He didn't. God has let me down. My season of nothing is getting intense! God, where are You?* Have you been there? I have.

Let's look together at Genesis 22:9: "When they reached the place God had told him about, Abraham built an altar there and arranged the wood on it. He bound his son Isaac and laid him on the altar, on top of the wood." Let's remember that Isaac knew the drill. He had been through this before. He realized what was going to happen to him. He had seen that knife cut through many animals, and now it was going to happen to him. I cannot imagine the screaming and begging: "Daddy, no! I love you, Dad! Don't hurt me! You are my hero, Dad!"

In Genesis 22:10–13, the Bible records:

Then he reached out his hand and took the knife to slay his son. But the angel of the Lord called out to him from heaven, "Abraham! Abraham!"

"Here I am," he replied.

"Do not lay a hand on the boy," he said. "Do not do anything to him. Now I know that you fear God, because you have not withheld from me your son, your only son."

Abraham looked up, and there in the thicket he saw a ram caught by its horns. He took the ram and sacrificed it as a burnt offering in place of his son.

Sometimes our seasons of nothing may take us all the way to the end. The battle gets intense, and we even sometimes feel as though our God has deserted us. But He always shows up just in time; He has a reputation for doing that! At times we feel like we have been taken to our limit, but if we keep trusting in Jesus, He will surely provide.

In the year 2000, we began to help raise the financing for church plants in the country of Ukraine. God helped us, and many people partnered with us for the cause. One of the places where we planted a church was a small village called Dniprilstan. Though it has only two hundred residents, we have never let size determine where we plant. I believe every town, city, and village deserves a church.

We planted this church in 2005, and I was privileged to return later to check on the church. They have had their share of setbacks, but the Lord continues to bless them. On my last visit there, five Ukrainian grandmothers followed me to the van as we were leaving. They stopped me and said through my interpreter that they were so grateful we had helped them get this church in their village. What they said next stunned me. One of the ladies acted as spokesperson for the group and said, "We are thankful because we [pointing at the other women] have been praying about this for fifty years." Fifty years—wow! Fifty years of nothing, and then God provided!

I know you may feel like you are on the other side of courageous and that God has forgotten you, but keep trusting in Him. Your season of nothing is coming to an end.

Reach for Jesus!
Listen to Jesus!
Trust in Jesus!
God is for you!

Questions for Discussion:

1. Are you currently in a season of nothing? How long have you been in this season?
2. Are you discouraged about your season of nothing? Are you thinking about giving up?
3. What is your greatest challenge in your season of nothing? What makes this challenge so difficult?
4. Are you currently reaching, listening, and trusting Jesus in this season of nothing?
5. Have you experienced another season of nothing, and did God show up in it? How did that affect your faith level?

HEALTHY FAMILY RELATIONSHIPS

I know I am not the only person to end up on the other side of courageous because of a relational disaster in life. I learned a lot from my failed marriage. One of the biggest things I learned was the importance of maintaining healthy family relationships. It is not only important, but it is vital. Do it!

When I was a kid, I loved to throw darts. I had some really close calls until I learned how to hit the board. My next goal was to hit the bull's-eye. Though I never achieved much success in reaching my goal, it was sure fun trying. I am just glad I never stabbed anyone with those darts!

I am going to use the circles on that dartboard as an analogy here. You see, God is the core (bull's-eye) of all relationships. We must realize going forward that this is the most important relationship that must be maintained in the life of a Christ-follower. Every other relationship springs from this one. If our relationship with God is not good, it affects our relationship with others. Likewise, if our relationship with others is not good, it affects our relationship with God. The core of our relational dartboard is God. "Seek first the kingdom of God . . ." (Matt. 6:33).

After God, our families come next. I will place them in the middle circle. In my trials, I have learned some important things about family life. I am going to be very basic as I share them with you, partly because I feel that is part of our problem: we have gotten away from our basic core beliefs.

1. IMPORTANCE OF THE FAMILY

God created the family before He created the church. I believe that building strong families is very vital to the church, though. Our churches will only be as strong as the families that make them up. We can point our fingers in a lot of directions and say *that* would make our church stronger. The truth is, if we build a strong church but our families are falling apart, we are not a strong church. That is part of the reason that almost every lead pastor I know does a series on the family every year.

SINGLES

Let me digress for a moment and address the growing number of single adults in our society. I did not marry the first time until I was thirty-five years old. I was married for three and a half years and single for seven more before Dianna and I married. Needless to say, I have spent a lot of time as a single adult. I know what it is to feel like the "third person" or the "fifth wheel."

Honestly, though, being single never bothered me much. I know several single adults who do not even like to go out in public unless they are with a group of people. It never bothered me to go out to eat alone or even to catch a movie by myself. Some people did stare at me, but I could never figure out if they felt sorry for me or were wishing they were me! There is something much worse than being single and wishing you were married, and that is being married and wishing you were single.

I really loved it when I would go out to eat alone, and the host or hostess would magnify their voice and say, "Party of one!" It was like they were saying, "Okay, everyone, look at this dude. He cannot get a date." I especially loved the word *party* there. Oh yeah, big party it was with me, myself and I!

I want every single adult to know that you have value. Everyone has value in God's eyes. You may have been rejected, but that does not make you a reject. You may be single, but you represent a family unit.

As a result of spending a lot of time as a single adult, I have been invited to speak at several singles' conferences through the years. One of the observations I have made is that singles often equate their life problems with being single. Dear single friend, you do not have problems because you are single; you have problems because you are a person. People have problems. When you get married, your problems do not vanish, but merely change. (I just heard a chuckle from the married crowd!)

I want to encourage you as a single adult not to spend your time looking for the right person, but rather spend your time *being* the right person. When you become the right person, God will send the right person to you. You are special in the eyes of God.

2. STRUCTURE OF THE FAMILY

    a. Dads/husbands—A couple of portions of Scripture really stand out to me as the Word of God establishes the role of the husband in the family structure.

        First is Ephesians 5:25–28: "Husbands, love your wives just as Christ loved the church and gave himself up for her to make her holy, cleansing her by the washing with water through the word, and to present her to himself as a radiant church, without stain or wrinkle or any other blemish, but holy and blameless. In this same way, husbands ought to love their wives as their own bodies. He who loves his wife loves himself."

Second is 1 Peter 3:7: "Husbands, in the same way be considerate as you live with your wives and treat them with respect as the weaker partner and as heirs with you of the gracious gift of life, so that nothing will hinder your prayers."

I am calling on all men of God to rise up from the other side of courageous and become the husbands and fathers God wants them to be. Men, work on your family relationships, and you, sir, lead your family into spiritual greatness! You can get promoted to the top and make all the money in the world, but if you lose your family, you have missed it.

b. Mom/wives—The Scripture passage that I want to share here is found in Ephesians 5:22–24: "Wives, submit yourselves to your husbands as to the Lord. For the husband is the head of the wife as Christ is the head of the church, his body, of which he is the Savior. Now as the church submits to Christ, so also wives should submit to their husbands in everything."

Let me take a moment and define submission. The subject is very delicate, but Scripture is very clear. In biblical submission, one equal voluntarily submits to another equal so that God will be glorified. Wives, submitting does not mean you are less than your husbands. All relationships have times when submission is required by all parties involved.

Raise your hand if you have ever noticed that men and women are different.

We do not have the time to go in to all the differences; however, I did come across something recently that I thought was humorous. My wife and I both laughed when we read this:

THE HAIRCUT

WOMAN 1: You got a haircut! That's so cute!

WOMAN 2: Do you think so? I wasn't sure when she gave me the mirror. I mean, you don't think it's too fluffy looking?

WOMAN 1: Oh no! It's perfect. I'd love to get my hair cut like that, but I think my face is too wide. I'm pretty much stuck with this stuff, I think.

WOMAN 2: Are you serious? I think your face is adorable. And you could easily get one of those layer cuts—that would look so cute on you. I was actually going to do that except that I was afraid it would accent my long neck.

WOMAN 1: Oh—that's funny! I would love to have your neck! Anything to take away from this two by four I have for a shoulder line.

WOMAN 2: Are you kidding? I know girls that would love to have your shoulders. Everything drapes so well on you. I mean, look at my arms; see how short they are? If I had your shoulders, I could get clothes to fit me so much easier.

A man' s version of the same haircut:

MAN 1: Haircut?
MAN 2: Yeah.

That's just one example of the way men and women are different!

c. Children—I encourage all children to be respectful, helpful, and thoughtful. It will take them so much further in life than the opposite of those things.

Atmosphere and *authority structure* often set the tone for maintaining healthy relationships. That leads me to my final point.

3. MAINTENANCE OF THE FAMILY

I call the following questions "assessing the details of your home." In connection with that, there are seven questions I want to ask you:

a. Do you compromise your standards or beliefs when unbelievers visit in your home?
   • Do you change your conversation or skip the prayer over your meal?

b. Do you require obedience from your children?

- Several years ago, the Duke of Windsor visited the United States. As he was boarding his plane to leave our country, a New York reporter asked him, "What was the thing that impressed you most about the United States?" The duke replied, "The thing that impressed me most about the United States is the way that parents obey their children!" Ouch! That is sad but true in our great country.

- Don't forget that your children are a blessing. They are your heritage, not a hindrance; a blessing, not a burden.

- Don't let your children run your house. That interrupts the authority structure and will eventually bring chaos (more on that in another chapter). Proverbs 22:6 says, "Train a child in the way he should go, and when he is old, he will not turn from it." The operative word here is *train*. There is a difference between raising children and training them. They cannot just grow up under your roof—you must train them. That involves setting up rules and guidelines. Do not allow your children to talk back. Make them go to church. Monitor what they watch. Parents, *you* train them. Someday they will love you for it!

- Don't neglect your children. Don't neglect to spend time with them (quantity and quality), and certainly don't neglect their spiritual needs. There is a difference between churchgoing parents and Christ- following parents.

c. Do you tolerate lying and deception in your home?
   - I want to encourage all parents to create a safe place for communication in their homes. Tell your kids they can talk about *anything* at home. It is a safe place! With that it mind, let them know that lying and deception are not tolerated and that there will be consequences with God and with you if they do— period.

d. Do you speak blessings or curses in your home?
   - Proverbs 18:21 says, "The tongue has the power of life and death." Speak life! I encourage that everywhere, but especially in the home.

- Spouses should bless each other with encouragement and compliments and speak blessings over their children. Refer back to my chapter "Sticks and Stones" for how harmful critical words can be.

e. Are there any addictions that have power over you?
  - If you are addicted to anything, break that bondage today! That addiction may be more powerful than you, but it is not more powerful than Jesus.

f. Are any forms of astrology tolerated in your home?
  - Christ-followers do not need to rely on such things. We serve the King of Kings and Lord of Lords!

g. Are there any obscene materials or movies in your home?
  - Job said he made a covenant with his eyes (Job 31:1), and you must do the same.
  - Inappropriate movies and materials will have serious repercussions in the long run. Remove them now.

Any of the things mentioned above will affect the atmosphere in our homes, which will in turn affect our relationships. If we give the devil a foothold, he will turn it into a stronghold. Let's not even let him set foot in our homes!

My pastor has been a great friend of mine for years. Pastor Randy Long and I met in Bible college and have been close friends ever since. He stood with me during my storm, and I will never forget his encouragement and support. Randy pastors Church Alive in Conway, Arkansas. I attend church there when I am not on the road.

One of the things Pastor Randy promotes consistently at Church Alive is what he calls "home worship." It is a simple concept but has proven powerful for us and others. It is simply as follows:

1. Pray together.
2. Read God's Word together.
3. Do communion together.

Try it consistently and watch God work in the atmosphere of your home. It will help your relationships too. God is the core of our lives and relationships. If He is glorified in our homes, He will help our family relationships be what He wants them to be.

Questions for Discussion:

1. Do you have consistent family devotions? Why or why not?
2. Have you ever read the scriptures on communion and taken communion together in your home? If so, describe what it was like.

3. What are the dangers of allowing things in your home that God would not be pleased with?
4. What do you do when you discover something has entered your home that you or God does not approve of?
5. After reading this chapter, are you prompted to make any changes in your home? If so, which changes will you make and why?

ALL YOU NEED IS LOVE

*Y*ou probably did a double take on the title of this chapter. Maybe you looked at that title and thought, *All I need? Wait a minute. I do not need only one thing; I need a lot of things!* Most of us cannot narrow down our needs to just one thing.

Then there is the word *love*. We all have different thoughts and feelings about that word. For teenagers, it may be a reference to those butterflies they feel in their stomach when they are around a certain person. Teenagers also believe that when they pull up to a stop sign while on a date, the letters *STOP* stand for "Smooch Till Others Pass"! Other people believe that love is a feeling and that the feeling will never change. However, love is not just a feeling—it is a decision.

For some people, the word *love* does not have a good meaning. Someone once told them they "loved" them, but then cheated on them or walked out of their lives. For those who have experienced that, I am so sorry. Some have had those who "love" them lie to them and deceive them, and they are thinking, *If that is what love is, I do not want any part of it!*

Regardless of where you are with the word *love*, I can say with full confidence that *all you need is love!* I can say that because of what the Word says in 1 John 4:16: "And so we know and rely on the love God has for us. God is love. Whoever lives in love lives in God, and God in him." Please focus on the words in the middle of that verse: "God is love." True, we do need a lot of things, but most of all, we need God, and God is love. If you are on the other side of courageous, feeling like everyone has forgotten you and that nobody loves you, know that God loves you. In fact, I want you to know that wherever you are and whatever you are doing right now, you are in the middle of God's love.

Ephesians 3:17–18 says, "And I pray that you, being rooted and established in love, may have power, together with all the saints, to grasp how wide and long and high and deep is the love of Christ." God's love is high, long, deep, and wide, and you are right in the middle of it. Here are a few other things I want you to know about God's love:

1. GOD'S LOVE PRODUCES JOY.

> "As the Father has loved me, so have I loved you. Now remain in my love. If you obey my commands, you will remain in my love, just as I have obeyed my Father's commands and remain in his love. I have told you this so that my joy may be in you and that your joy may

be complete" (John 15:9–11). God's love produces joy!

There is a difference between joy and happiness. I am not happy when my favorite sports team loses, but it does not affect my joy in Jesus. I also want you realize that the joy of Jesus is a real source of strength in our lives. As Nehemiah 8:10 proclaims, "The joy of the Lord is our strength."

Be released from the bondage of trying to make everyone happy. It is a never-ending cycle and is impossible to achieve. Church leaders cannot do it, bosses cannot do it, parents cannot do it—you simply cannot make everyone happy. When you do right things and stand for right things, some will not be happy about it.

Remember what Mark Twain said about joy: "Some people spread joy wherever they go; other people spread joy whenever they go." Which describes you?

2. GOD'S LOVE DEVELOPS A WINNER'S MENTALITY.

"Who shall separate us from the love of Christ? Shall trouble or hardship or persecution or famine or nakedness or danger or sword? . . . No, in all these things we are more than conquerors through him who loved us" (Rom. 8:35–37).

Through Christ you are a winner, more than a conqueror. Even on the other side of courageous, God has conquerors!

3. GOD'S LOVE IS DEMONSTRATED TO US.

"For God so loved the world that he gave his one and only Son, that whoever believes in him shall not perish but have eternal life" (John 3:16). God did not just tell us He loves us—He demonstrated it. He sent His Son to die for our sins. He did not just talk the talk, but He walked the walk.

I came across a great illustration of a son demonstrating his love to his father. I'd like to share it with you:

Help in the Garden

An old Italian lived in New Jersey. He wanted to plant his annual tomato garden, but it was very difficult work, as the ground was hard. His only son, Vincent, who used to help him, was in prison. The old man wrote a letter to his son and described his predicament:

Dear Vincent,

I am feeling pretty sad because it looks like I won't be able to plant my tomato garden this year. I am just getting too old to be digging up a garden plot. I know if you were here, my troubles would be over. I know you would be happy to dig up the ground for me, like in the old days.

Love,
Papa

A few days later the father received a letter from his son:

Dear Pop,
Don't dig up that garden. That's where the bodies are buried.

Love,
Vinnie

At 4:00 a.m. the next morning, FBI agents and local police arrived and dug up the entire area without finding any bodies. They apologized to the old man and left. The same day the man received another letter from his son:

Dear Pop,

Go ahead and plant the tomatoes now. That's the best I could do under the circumstances.

I love you,
Vinnie

He sure demonstrated his love for his father, huh?

4. GOD'S LOVE IS DEMONSTRATED THROUGH US.

This point is not to be confused with my prior point, which was God's love is demonstrated *to* us.

"Dear children, let us not love with words or tongue but with actions and truth. This is how we know that we belong to the truth, and how we set our hearts at rest in his presence whenever our hearts condemn us. For God is greater than our hearts and he knows everything" (1 John 3:18–20).

God's love is demonstrated through us in the way we live and the way we treat others. I want to show God's love today!

5. GOD'S LOVE CANNOT BE TAKEN AWAY FROM US.

"Neither height nor depth, nor anything else in all creation, will be able to separate us from the love of God that is in Christ Jesus our Lord" (Rom. 8:39).

Nothing can separate you from His love. I have talked to so many people who ask, "How can God love me after all I have done?" He just does. *Nothing* can separate you from that love. On the other side of courageous, that is sometimes hard to see, but know for a fact that He loves you!

Questions for Discussion:

1. Is it really possible to grasp how much God loves us? Discuss.
2. We have learned that God's love produces joy in our lives. Do you *really* have the joy of Jesus in you? Explain your answer.
3. What are some ways that God's love is demonstrated *to* us?
4. What are some ways that God's love is demonstrated *through* us?
5. Has there ever been a time in your life when you felt like God no longer loved you? What made you feel this way?

LIVING ON LEFTOVERS

I grew up in church back in the . . . well, let's just say a long time ago. When I was a kid, it was normal for my family to have people over for a meal on Sunday after the morning service. Restaurants were not as big of a deal then as they are now, so growing up, we had most of our meals at home.

One of the many great childhood memories I have are the times when we had company over for meals. Since we were Christians, we could not possibly get together without having food! My mom was (and still is) a great cook. For the sake of illustration, let me use ham as an example.

My mom would fix a nice, juicy ham, and we would all pig out (no pun intended). Seriously, though, we would attack that ham. We would all eat until we were stuffed and could not hold any more. However, even after giving it our best shot, we could never finish that ham. There was always some left, which was great with me because the leftover ham always made a good sandwich.

Like most teenagers, I could eat. I could put the food away with the best of them. If you have raised kids or currently have kids in your house, you know they can put the groceries away during the teen years and beyond. Most teens eat their cereal out of satellite dishes instead of bowls!

However, there was some food I could hardly eat. School food fell in that category. When I went to Bible college, the cafeteria food was less than desirable. We students always said that they could do more things with noodles than we had ever seen in our lives.

Anyway, in high school, I would come home in the afternoon, and the first words out of my mouth would be, "Mom, do we have anything to eat?" Well, on the Monday after the Sunday that we had enjoyed ham, Mom would say, "Lynn, there is some ham left from yesterday." Yes! It sure made a good ham sandwich the day after it was first served.

However, the process soon repeated itself because I was always hungry. If I came in on Tuesday and asked for something to eat, and my mom said to me again, "Lynn there is still ham left from Sunday," I was not as excited this time. In fact, I would complain, though that never got me far. Every time I complained, my mom would merely say the same thing to me. I think it is written in a mom's book somewhere, because I know several moms who said the same thing my mom would say to me: "You can have that or do without." Whoa! I certainly couldn't do without. I was sure I would die of malnutrition, so reluctantly I ate ham three days in a row.

However, if I came in on Wednesday and got the same response from Mom, now I was done. I loved ham, but not four days in a row! It was great on Sunday, it was good on Monday, I endured it on Tuesday, but now I was done with ham for a while. Why? Because we all like variety. We do not want the same thing to eat every day.

This story brings me to a question that will help us get back to the courageous side. If we refuse to live on leftovers in the natural, why do we have a tendency to do it spiritually? I hear people talking all the time about what "God used to do" or "what He did back when" or "how my life was changed in a revival in 1999." Don't get me wrong. I rejoice in what the Lord did in days gone by. I am in no way lessening what God did then, but what God did then, He wants to do today. The good news is that you do not have to live on spiritual leftovers! God is the same yesterday, today, and forever.

I love the way Paul put it to the church in Corinth: "Therefore we do not lose heart. Though outwardly we are wasting away, inwardly we are being renewed day by day" (2 Cor. 4:16). Inward, *daily* renewal keeps us from living on spiritual leftovers. God has something new and fresh for us every day of our lives.

When talking about the Word of God, Joshua said, "Meditate on it day and night" (Josh. 1:8). The psalmist said to "proclaim his salvation day after day" (Ps. 96:2).

We all have heard the prayer in the Bible that is called the Lord's Prayer. In fact, probably many of you have memorized that prayer. One of the places this prayer is recorded in Scripture is Luke 11. This prayer came from Jesus in response to a request that one of His disciples asked of him: "Lord, teach us to pray" (v. 1).

I want to focus on a particular part of that prayer. Jesus said in verse 3 for us to pray, "Give us each day our daily bread." The Lord encourages us to pray *daily* for *daily* bread. Keeping your relationship with the Lord updated and fresh is key when you are on the other side of courageous.

In the Old Testament, the daily bread referred to was manna. Let's look at a portion of Scripture in Exodus 16:11–20:

> The Lord said to Moses, "I have heard the grumbling of the Israelites. Tell them, 'At twilight you will eat meat and in the morning you will be filled with bread. Then you will know that I am the Lord your God.'"
>
> That evening quail came and covered the camp, and in the morning there was a layer of dew around the camp. When the dew was gone, thin flakes like frost on the ground appeared on the desert floor. When the Israelites saw it, they said to each other, "What is it?" For they that did not know what it was.
>
> Moses said to them, "It is the bread the Lord has given you to eat. This is what the Lord has commanded: 'Each one is to gather as much as he needs. Take an omer for each person you have in your tent.'"

The Israelites did as they were told; some gathered much, some little. And when they measured it by the omer, he who gathered much did not have too much, and he who had gathered little did not have too little. Each one gathered as much as he needed.

Then Moses said to them, "No one is to keep any of it until morning."

However, some of them paid no attention to Moses; they kept part of it until morning, but it was full of maggots and began to smell. So Moses was angry with them.

The verse I want to focus on is verse 20: "No one is to keep any of it until morning." My interpretation of that is *no leftovers!*

I want to stop and give you some reasons why I do not like leftovers:

1. LEFTOVERS DO NOT SOUND GOOD.

When Mom said "ham" for a fourth day in a row, it did not sound good at all. I wanted something new and fresh. In the same way, I want new and fresh sounds coming from our worship experiences. Let me explain. Every time we come together in worship, I so long to hear things like, "Lord, forgive me; I am a sinner," or "I was healed in service today." I want those to be *daily* sounds coming from the church!

In Acts 2, the disciples in the upper room experienced God in a powerful way. That entire experience started with a sound: "Suddenly there came a sound from heaven" (Acts 2:2). I want God to speak things to me that He has never spoken before. I call those *fresh* sounds from heaven.

2. LEFTOVERS DO NOT LOOK GOOD.

Another reason I do not like leftovers is that after a while, they do not look good. What on Sunday had been a nice, juicy ham by Wednesday was merely a glob of unappetizing meat. It didn't look nearly as good as it did when it was fresh.

I encourage you not to live on spiritual leftovers. With everything in me, I ask you to keep God fresh in your daily life. One of the reasons I am passionate about this is that I have seen what happens when people do not do this. If you live on spiritual leftovers long enough, the church soon loses its attractiveness to you. It does not have the same appeal as before. It is at this point that many people become critical (refer to chapter "Sticks and Stones").

3. LEFTOVERS DO NOT TASTE GOOD.

Taste is the deciding factor. Many times I have put some leftovers into my mouth only to discover that the food did not taste the same. What tasted so good on Sunday by Wednesday was bland and undesirable. In fact, I might put it into my mouth and chew . . . and chew . . . and chew . . . and chew. Sometimes I chewed so long I actually became afraid to put *that* in my stomach!

"Taste and see that God is good," says Psalm 34:8. I encourage you to do so *daily!*

4. LEFTOVERS GET MOLD ALL OVER THEM.

Have you ever seen something that has been left in the refrigerator too long? Sometimes it looks like green and brown furry creatures have attached themselves to that food. Yuck! I do not know how they get in there, but they do. At this point, it doesn't matter if the leftover food was your favorite food—you are not touching it. It has become totally unappealing.

I had an experience a few years ago with molded food. I left the country on a missions trip for twelve days. At that time, I was single and lived alone. When I got home and looked in my fridge, I discovered that I had left tuna salad in there. It was in one of those containers that you cannot see through, and it had gotten pushed to the back of the fridge. When I opened the container to examine the contents, both the sight and smell were quite repulsive. Whew! It was one of those times when you do not throw out only the food, but the whole container as well, because nothing could ever live in that container again!

One of the things that happens to us if we live on leftovers is that something will attach itself to us, too. It is not mold—it is sin! If we cannot get our daily bread from heaven, our ability to fight temptation is compromised. If we do not have spiritual manna strengthening us, we weaken spiritually. And it's just when we are at our weakest that the enemy attacks the hardest.

Stay strong! Fight the enemy with a fresh experience with God every day. Meet with God and talk to Him. Let Him speak to you. Read His Word and get it in your spirit.

Mold on food will eventually destroy the food. It takes out every ounce of nutritional value that was intended to build our bodies. In a similar fashion, sin destroys us spiritually. It takes out all the spiritual vitamins that give us strength to fight the enemy. So I say to you, no leftovers! Fresh manna!

Now let's go back to Exodus 16 before we close this chapter. Something here really surprises me. The Lord had given specific instructions to not keep any of the manna until morning. However, verse 20 says, "Some of them paid no attention to Moses; they kept part of it until morning, but it was full of maggots and began to smell."

Why would the people of God openly disobey Him? The Lord said "don't," but they did. What the Lord had sent to give them nourishment turned into molded bread that smelled bad. It was all tied to disobedience.

To get back to the courageous side of things will require obedience on your part—not partial obedience, but complete obedience. My challenge to you is to walk in that obedience, feasting on the *daily bread* from heaven. You do not have to live on leftovers; God has something fresh for you today. It will give you the strength to get back to the courageous side in your life!

Questions for Discussion:

1. Do you have a daily time with Jesus? When is it, and what do you do?
2. Do you read God's Word daily? Why is that so important?
3. Have you gone through a season in your life when you were spiritually living on leftovers? Describe the situation. Are you still there? Explain.
4. Why is it dangerous to live on past spiritual experiences? What is the end result of that?
5. Do you have a goal of making sure you do not end up living on leftovers? What are the steps you will take to make sure the "mold" does not attach itself to you?

THE BIG *I*

A few years ago, I made a trip through the drive-through window of my bank. That is at least a weekly errand for me; thus it has become a fairly routine part of my schedule. I live in a small town where the bank calls me by name when I pull up to the window. I usually make the necessary transaction and drive off to do other errands. When I am home, this process is just routine for me.

One day I went through the usual process, making my transaction and receiving the cash that I had requested. My next stop was in a town about fifteen miles away. This was the dreaded Walmart stop. I say "dreaded" because this store, quite honestly, is not my favorite place. Anyway, I went in, got the things I needed, and proceeded to the checkout line. When I pulled out my money to pay, I noticed that the bank had given me an extra two hundred dollars in my cash-back transaction. Needless to say, I was shocked. I knew this bank teller and knew she had made an honest mistake. It was going to be a few hours before I could get back to the bank, and I knew she would notice that some money was missing and not even know what had happened to it.

Can I tell you that for the next three hours, the enemy spoke loud and often to me: "It is only two hundred dollars." . . . "You know you could use an extra two hundred dollars right now." . . . "It's not like you stole it; she gave it to you." Those are the phrases that kept running through my mind. I heard what was being said, but I never took the bait. My integrity was worth more to me than a mere two hundred dollars. In fact, integrity does not have a price tag—not ever. You and I must never allow ourselves to be bought by money or fame. Doing right is more important than appearing right publicly.

I returned the money to the bank. When I walked in, I could see the teller in the corner with an adding machine and several papers. She was frantically trying to find the two hundred dollars that was missing from her books. I called her over and gave her the money. The relief on her face was priceless. Had I not returned the funds, she would have had to pay it out of her own pocket. Doing the right thing felt good. God has and will always honor the right things we do.

Oh yeah, the big *I* . . . the must in everyone's life. The compass that guides us is called *integrity*. The dictionary defines integrity as "a reputation of trustworthiness that is built up over a period of time and is proven by our behavior and conduct both in the public view as well as when nobody is looking." Wow! I think we can all admit to integrity lapses in our lives, but going forward, let's make a commitment to maintain our integrity. It is the big *I*.

It may be a lapse in integrity that has taken some of you to the other side of courageous. If that is the case, stay the course. It will take time to rebuild trust, but it *can* be done.

In his book *Why Great Men Fall*, Wayde Goodall says the following: "When Warren Buffett, CEO of Berkshire Hathaway, chooses people to lead in his organization, he says, 'In looking for people to hire, you look for three qualities: integrity, intelligence, and energy. If you don't have the first, the other two will kill you.' Buffet goes on to say, 'It takes twenty years to build a reputation and five minutes to ruin it. If you think about that, you will do things differently."(1) It sounds like the big *I* (integrity) is a must to work in his organization.

Proverbs 25:26 says, " Like a muddied spring or a polluted well is a righteous man who gives way to the wicked." Compromising your integrity is the first step in destroying yourself and those close to you. That is why the enemy works overtime to put temptations in your path. He wants to cause you to stumble and fall, and your fall *will* affect others as well.

Look at what Paul wrote: "So, if you think you are standing firm, be careful that you don't fall. No temptation has seized you except what is common to man. And God is faithful; he will not let you be tempted beyond what you can bear. But when you are tempted, he will also provide a way out so that you can stand up under it" (1 Cor. 10:12–13). There is a way out! When you are under attack from the enemy of your soul, find the escape route. God says there is one, but it is up to you to find it.

I want to look at a couple of people in the Bible and examine their responses to temptation. They are great examples of the big *I*.

First, let's look at a man named Samson. Samson knew what it was to have the Spirit of the Lord on him. In fact, three different times in Judges 14 and 15, the Bible says, "The Spirit of the Lord came upon him in power" (Judg. 14:6, 19; 15:14). However, knowing what it is to have the Spirit of the Lord on you does not mean you will never face opportunities to compromise your integrity. Sadly, many great men have fallen because they thought that the presence of the Spirit of the Lord on their lives was equal to a life of integrity. Samson exposes this assumption as a myth.

In Judges 16, we find Samson in the valley of Sorek, in love with a prostitute named Delilah (v. 4). The rulers of the Philistines saw that Samson had fallen for her and offered Delilah a lot of money if she could get him to reveal the secret of his strength (v. 5). So Delilah tried to discover the secret, but on three different occasions, Samson lied to her (vv. 7, 11, and 13). Each time she followed through with what he said and cooperated in a plot to kill him. *Three times* he compromised his life; yet, unbelievably, he continued to put his head in Delilah's lap.

Finally, Samson told Delilah the truth (v. 17), and the destruction began. He ended up in prison, his eyes plucked out (v. 21). The Philistines rejoiced over his fall, and some time later they requested that Samson be brought from prison to entertain them. Samson requested to be placed between the pillars of the building, and the request was granted. His strength returned, and he pushed mightily on the pillars until the entire temple crashed down, killing more than three thousand people in the process. Samson, too, died that day (vv. 23–30).

Please notice that Samson's problems started because he continued to lay his head in the lap of Delilah. She burned him three times, but he never learned his lesson. In this case, a lack of integrity cost him his life. What a sad ending.

The other person I want to talk about is Joseph. We discussed him in the chapter on forgiveness, but there are so many great things we can learn from his life. I want to take you to a place in his life that is recorded in Genesis 39.

As a result of being sold into slavery by his brothers, Joseph ended up working for a man named Potiphar, one of Pharaoh's officials in Egypt. Joseph was a "well built and handsome man" (v. 6), and Potiphar's wife began to take notice of him. Day after day she tried to entice Joseph into a sexual encounter, and day after day he refused (v. 10).

Then one day she literally grabbed Joseph by his cloak, begging him to come to bed with her. Instead, he ran out of the house (v. 12). She was so angry that she made up a lie and told her husband that Joseph had tried to rape her (vv. 17–18). Potiphar was so angry that he threw Joseph into prison (v. 20). Joseph did the right thing and ended up in prison for it!

Sometimes you cannot control the actions and words of others, but you will never go wrong by doing the right thing. Let's continue with our story to prove my point.

I love this verse: "But while Joseph was in prison, the Lord was with him; he showed him kindness and granted him favor in the eyes of the prison warden." Joseph was *favored* by God while in a place he should never have been. It was not his fault that he was in prison, so despite everything, the Lord favored him. God is good! I love it! Everywhere Joseph went, he was promoted. Integrity does pay off in the end. Let's continue.

In chapter 40, God gave Joseph some interpretations to dreams, and Pharaoh began to take notice. Then another promotion came in Genesis 41:39–40: "Then Pharaoh said to Joseph, 'Since God has made all this known to you, there is no one so discerning and wise as you. You shall be in charge of my palace, and all my people are to submit to your orders. Only with respect to the throne will I be greater than you."

Wow! Joseph went from being second in Potiphar's house to second in Pharaoh's court. What a promotion! Granted, it was a long road that included time in prison, but he came out of prison with his integrity intact. Joseph's story is proof that no one can take our integrity from us. If we lose it, it is because we laid it down. Joseph refused to lay his down.

The stories are becoming all too common of people who are laying down their integrity. Politicians, athletes, coaches, ministers, and many others are implicated. I want to ask you some very serious questions today. These might be a gauge for your integrity compass. Please answer honestly.

1. Are you more concerned about what you are than *who* you are?

   If so, you might be on a path to compromising integrity. Who you are is more important than what you are and what you do. If you will work on the *who*, God will take care of the *what*.

2. Are you struggling with unrevealed secret sin?

   Do not believe the lie that just because a certain sin has not been revealed, it must be harmless. That sin has put you on a dangerous path. Deal with it today. Get it under the blood of Jesus and walk away. One minister said it like this: "Admit it—quit it—forget it." I like that!

3. Who are the people that you are accountable to?

   I believe in accountability. I have had an accountability partner for years. I also know that accountability is only as strong as the honesty revealed. If you have an accountability partner or group, but you are not honest in that relationship, it is null and void.

Honesty is a must in the area of integrity. Nobody can help you if you are not honest. Be honest before God and man.

If you would like to have an accountability partner but do not know how to get one, maybe these things will help:

a. Look for someone who loves you and believes in you. There should be no doubt about it—they do!
b. Look for someone you know you can trust.
c. Look for someone who will not judge you because of the struggles you are having.
d. Look for someone to whom you are comfortable granting permission to ask you anything at any time.
e. Look for someone who is a God-fearing person.

Some people prefer an accountability group to an accountability partner. I know of several men's accountability groups that meet for breakfast. The meeting is a safe place where struggles can be shared. Whatever you are more comfortable with is what I encourage you to do. Just do it! (I know, phrase not original!) It will help you in the area of integrity.

"The man of integrity walks securely, but he who takes crooked paths will be found out," declares Proverbs 10:9. Partial integrity is not acceptable. Being a person of integrity in one area, but not in another will eventually catch up with you. Several years ago, I read a great book by Charles Swindoll called *Strengthening Your Grip*. In that book, he reveals a great story that illustrates my point well:

Some time ago, I heard about a fellow in Long Beach who went into a fried chicken franchise to get some chicken for himself and the young lady with him. She waited in the car while he went in to pick up the chicken. Inadvertently, the manager of the store handed the guy the box in which he had placed the financial proceeds of the day instead of the box of chicken. You see, he was going to make a deposit and had camouflaged it by putting money in a fried chicken box.

The fellow took his box, went back to the car, and the two of them drove away. When they got to the park and opened the box, they discovered they had a box full of money. Now that's a very vulnerable moment for the average individual. He realized there must have been a mistake, so he got back in his car and returned to the place and gave the money back to the manager. Well, the manager was elated! He was so pleased that he told the young man, "Stick around. I want to call the newspaper and have them take your picture. You're the most honest guy in town."

"Oh no! Don't do that!" said the fellow.

"Why not?" asked the manager.

"Well," he said, "you see, I'm married, and the woman I am with is not my wife." (2)

Partial integrity? Integrity in one area of your life but not in another? It will eventually go full circle.

Friend, if you have integrity issues, please resolve them. You cannot lead or help others until your personal life is in order. Make it a priority to never sell out the big *I*. It is part of the process of getting back to courageous.

Questions for Discussion:

1. What are the consequences of a lapse in integrity?
2. Why is harboring secret sin such a dangerous practice?
3. Do you have an accountability partner? Are you completely honest with your partner on every level?
4. What are some scriptural examples of people who compromised their integrity? What happened to them?
5. Have you ever seen something positive happen as a result of you maintaining your integrity? Please share.

ALL STRESSED UP AND NO PLACE TO GO

I t is not a new revelation: we all know these are high-stress days that we're living in. Oh, I know, I've heard all the church rhymes too, like "I'm too blessed to be stressed!" It sure sounds good, and we have already established that we are a blessed people. However, most of us live under a cloud of stress that we rarely get relief from. I vote we all vacation every other week. Who's in?

It really does not matter which side of courageous you are on; there is going to be stress in your life. Whether you live in a traditional family unit or a blended family, there will be stress. The Bible addresses the subject by the use of the words *anxious* and *anxiety*:

"Cast all your anxiety on him, for he cares for you" (1 Pet. 5:7).

"An anxious heart weighs a man down, but a kind word cheers him up" (Prov. 12:25)

"Do not be anxious about anything, but in everything, with prayer and petition, with thanksgiving, present your request to God" (Phil. 4:6).

I want to take some time in this chapter to discuss, in my opinion, the three main roots of stress. Please understand that I am not a doctor, nor do I play one on TV. These are just my observations from a spiritual perspective. But let's take a look at them and learn how to battle stress with God's Word:

1. WORRY

Worry is a root that grows into stress. Unfortunately, I encounter a lot of worry-bound believers in my travels. The grip of worry has them so confined that they can hardly function. You can even see the worry on their faces, because worry affects our countenances. But look at what Jesus said about worry in Matthew 6:25–34:

Therefore I tell you, do not worry about your life, what you will eat or drink; or about your body, what you will wear. Is not life more important than food and the body more important than clothes? Look at the birds of the air; they do not sow or reap or store away in barns, and yet your heavenly Father feeds them. Are you not much more valuable than they? Who of you by worrying can add a single hour to his life?

And why do you worry about clothes? See how the lilies of the field grow. They do not labor or spin. Yet I tell you that not even Solomon in all his splendor was dressed like one of these. If that is how God clothes the grass of the field, which is here today and tomorrow is thrown in to the fire, will he not much more clothe you, O you of little faith? So do not worry, saying, "What shall we eat?" or "What shall we drink?" or "What shall we wear?" For the pagans run after all these things, and your heavenly Father knows that you need them. But seek first his kingdom and his righteousness, and all these things will be given to you as well. Therefore do not worry about tomorrow, for tomorrow will worry about itself. Each day has enough trouble of its own.

I realize it is hard for us not to worry about our kids, our finances, our future, etc. I also know that God is still in control, and for us believers to agonize and worry does us no good. In fact, we have no control over most of the things we worry about, so it is pointless to do so. I encourage you today to let it go—God's got this! Remind yourself of what Jesus said in verse 27: "Who of you by worrying can add a single hour to his life?" The answer is obvious: none of us can!

Isaiah 26:3 promises, "You will keep in perfect peace him whose mind is steadfast, because he trusts in you." I pray peace over your mind right now. Worry has crippled you and affected your life. You cannot even sleep at night because worry has such a powerful hold on your mind. But, in Jesus' name, I am speaking peace to all those areas in your life where there has been worry. Amen! Tonight you will sleep better than you have in months!

2. DEPRESSION

I have never been actually diagnosed with depression, but I have been through it. I know what it is, and I know I have endured seasons of it in my life. On two different occasions, I sought counseling. The first time was an attempt to save my first marriage, and the second time was to help me deal with the aftereffects of my divorce, especially those things regarding my daughter.

While neither of these professional counselors ever diagnosed me with depression, and I never took medication for it, I recognize its deep, dark journey. In my struggle, my mind could not focus or think clearly. All I wanted to do was lie around and stare vacantly into space. When I tried to do things, even things I had previously enjoyed doing, it was like walking in mud. There was just no will or energy to go on.

Depression is a root of stress for many people, especially those on the other side of courageous. It is so hard to get going again after a failure in your life. I know this from personal experience. But I also know that while it is difficult, it is possible. Jesus said, "With man this is impossible, but not with God; all things are possible with God" (Mark 10:27).

The prophet Isaiah encourages us to "put on a garment of praise instead of a spirit of despair" (Isa. 61:3). Another version of the Bible calls it a "spirit of heaviness." Isaiah references that despair and heaviness are spirits. The dictionary defines *depressed* as "to be flattened vertically or dispirited." Any way you look at it, depression is a heavy force against mankind.

During the sentencing process of Jesus, the Scripture records that "soldiers twisted together a crown of thorns and put it on his head" (John 19:2). When the soldiers placed that crown on Jesus' head, He immediately began to bleed. The moment the thorns connected with the flesh on His head, blood began to flow.

I believe that the blood that flowed from Jesus' head can now be applied to our minds to bring us the healing we need. Depression, be lifted from the minds of God's people, in Jesus' name! If you need healing in your mind today, receive that. The blood of Jesus

177

never fails, not even on the other side of courageous.

3. FEAR

"For God did not give us a spirit of timidity, but of power and love and self-discipline" (2 Tim. 1:7). If God did not give us the spirit of fear, then who did? Again, it is the enemy of our soul trying to put us on a destructive course, but he will fail!

In Scripture, the phrase "do not be afraid" is recorded 366 times. The way I see it, that is one for each day of the year and one extra for leap year. So we are covered!

Fear is a very real and paralyzing tool of the enemy. I have seen and experienced all kinds of fears at different stages of my life. I shared in my first book, *Living Free,* about my fear of dogs. When I was six years old, my mom took me to the church one night while they were having a women's meeting. All the kids decided to play hide-and-seek. It was dark, and as I headed around the corner of the church, a German shepherd jumped on me and bit my leg. To this day, I still bear the scar, and I can still visualize that attack as clearly today as the day that it happened forty-five years ago. While time has helped, I still have my moments when I see a dog, especially a German shepherd.

The things we are afraid of are many and varied. I have seen a grown man freak out while boarding a plane because his fear of flying overwhelmed him. I have seen people scream and run at the sight of a spider. There are children *and* adults who are afraid of the dark. Fear of heights causes a lot of people to stay on the ground. Fear of other people cripples some in their social interactions. On and on we could go.

There are so many weapons of fear the enemy is using today. How can you fight fear? Your weapon against fear is faith. Speak to your fears through faith in God. Smother them by declaring what the Word of God says. You can be full of faith even on the other side of courageous. Fear adds so much stress to our lives, but I cancel it off your life today!

I cannot leave the subject of fear without talking about one particular healthy fear; that is, the fear of the Lord. I do not mean being afraid of God, but rather, possessing a reverence and awe of God. Psalm 111:10 says, "To fear the Lord is the beginning of wisdom." Here are some benefits of a healthy fear of the Lord:

a. Long life—"The fear of the Lord adds length to life" (Prov. 10:27).
b. Wisdom—"The fear of the Lord teaches a man wisdom" (Prov. 15:33).

c. Avoidance of evil—"Through the fear of the Lord, a man avoids evil" (Prov. 16:6).

Job was described as a man who "fears God and shuns evil" (Job 1:8). I want to be that man too!

A healthy fear of the Lord will bring strength and stability to your life, while other fears will destroy dreams and paralyze your progress. Today is a new beginning for you. Feed your faith and starve your fears! Faith will overpower your fears. Here are some ways to feed your faith:

a. Read your Bible daily (remember the chapter on leftovers).
b. Be faithful in your church attendance. There is value in worshiping with others in a corporate setting.
c. Listen to worship CDs and preaching or teaching CDs often. You cannot get too much of this.
d. Be involved in a small group where members build each other up.
e. Pray daily. Communication with God brings peace and faith.

If you are stressed out, build up your faith! Today is your day. You are on your way back to courageous, and stress cannot go with you!

Questions for Discussion:

1. Why do you believe the stress level is so high in our society today?
2. Do you personally struggle with worry? If so, how does it affect your everyday life?
3. What is your greatest fear? How does it paralyze you?
4. What are you currently doing to help overcome fear in your life?
5. What have you done lately to help relieve the stress in someone else's life?

THE AUTHORITY ISSUE

*T*he story is told of a farm inspector who showed up at the house of a farmer to inspect his farm. When the farmer opened door, the inspector showed him his card and said, "I am here to inspect your farm. This card gives me the authority to go anywhere on your farm and look around." Unimpressed, the farmer nodded his assent.

The inspector, still trying to impress the farmer, continued, "Do you understand? *This card* means I can go into your barn, look at your equipment, and check out your livestock." Again the farmer nodded nonchalantly.

Frustrated that the farmer was not impressed with his card and the authority it gave, the inspector continued, "Do you *really* understand that because of this card, I can literally go *anywhere* and do *anything* on your property?" Again the farmer gave a half-hearted nod.

Frustrated at his attempts to impress the farmer, the inspector began to walk through the farm. After a few minutes, the farmer heard a loud scream outside:

"Help! Help! Help!" He walked out onto the porch and noticed the inspector caught in the pen with the prize bull. The bull was coming at him hard, fast, and low.

While the inspector screamed frantically for help, the farmer yelled back from the porch, "Show him your card, man! Show him your card!"

We both know two things about this story:

a. The bull was *not* impressed by the inspector's card.
b. The card was not going to stop the bull from plowing into the inspector with full force.

So that which the inspector thought gave him authority was not effective. His authority was not all-inclusive. While it worked with the farmer, it did not work with the bull.

Authority is one of the most sensitive subjects to discuss. Authority issues promote power struggles, which wreak much damage. I have seen churches split, marriages fall apart, relationships disintegrate, and big companies stagnate over power struggles rooted in authority issues.

Let me remind you that when Satan fell from heaven, it was an authority issue: "And there was a war in heaven. Michael and his angels fought against the dragon, and the dragon and his angels fought back. But he was not strong enough, and they lost their place in heaven. The great dragon was hurled down—that ancient serpent called the devil, or

Satan, who leads the world astray. He was hurled to the earth and his angels with him" (Rev. 12:7–9).

Just a side note: I love the part in verse 8 that says, "But he was not strong enough." Satan was not strong enough to defeat heaven then, and he is not strong enough to defeat heaven now! The battle you are facing may be stronger than you, but it is not stronger than God.

Okay, back to the subject at hand: authority. As soon as this battle was over and heaven had declared victory, God's voice boomed through the heavens these words: "Now have come the salvation and the power of the kingdom of our God, and the *authority* of his Christ" (Rev. 12:10, emphasis added). At that moment, God's authority was established as priority in heaven and on earth. So we move forward on the subject of authority acknowledging that our God is and will always be the highest authority.

I have been a stepdad in two different marriages. In both marriages, my oldest stepsons made this statement to me at one time or another: "You are not my dad!" You guessed it—it was when I was telling them what to do. There is a very fine line to walk when you are the newcomer in a family. In my first marriage, the boy's father had passed away in an accident. In the second marriage, the dad still played a very active role in his son's life after divorce severed the relationship with the boy's mother.

I am going to divide my discussion of parenting or stepparenting into two categories: first of all, "my greatest mistakes," and second, "my greatest beliefs." Here we go! These were my greatest mistakes:

1. Thinking that parenting equals church leadership

   a. I was married for the first time at thirty-five years old. When I became a stepdad, I immediately began to parent these boys as though they were in my youth group. *Wrong!* Parenting requires a relationship on a deeper level. You cannot parent as though you and your kids are on a perpetual trip to Six Flags.
   b. In my second marriage, I have done much better, but I still have my moments. Parenting is always a work in progress.

2. Thinking that I had a better system than my spouse

   a. I did not have a *better* system; I had a *different* system. I learned that neither system was inherently right or wrong, but merely different.
   b. When children have been through the death of a parent or lost a parent through divorce, they do not need "different." It takes time to adjust. You must let them. You cannot force the process.

   Dianna and I married in March of 2006. After we returned from our honeymoon, reality set in. The first morning back, we were getting the boys ready for school. I jumped right in and began helping with breakfast, packing lunches, etc. I was the knight in shining armor—or so I thought—and they could rest easy now that I was here. *Baloney!*

I was going ninety miles an hour doing this and that. At one point, I finally looked up and saw the look on Dianna's face. I had interrupted their system. I was threatening their "normal," and nobody was handling it well. It broke my heart when I realized I was adding stress to the situation, so I backed off. Now I stay in the bedroom until everyone is out the door. Their system works for them, and I needed to let it.

3. Thinking that the children would automatically love me

   a. My mistake was in thinking that just because I had a love relationship with their mom, I would automatically have a good relationship with them too.
   b. In the area of being a stepdad, love comes from building trust with your stepchildren. Kids should always know they can trust the adults in their lives. Once trust is established, love will follow.
   c. Sometimes when you come into a family as a stepparent, the children view your presence as a threat. It appears to them as

if you are taking their mom or dad away from them. I failed to reassure my step-children in that area, and I do not want you to make the same mistake.

Second, I want to talk to you about my greatest beliefs. It was difficult to reduce this to three, but here is what I have come up with:

1. I still believe that *parents* are the ones in charge of the home.

    If the authority structure in the home is out of line, chaos will surely follow at some point. I see this all the time in public: children giving orders to their parents. One parent once said to me, "It is just easier that way." If you think that is true, be assured that the ease you feel now will certainly turn into hardship later. Do not take the easy way. Parenting is not and never will be easy.

2. I still believe there are absolutes in the home.

    As long as children live under your roof, you have a right to have and enforce rules. Obviously, those rules change with the children's age and maturity. However, as long as children live in your home, you can establish some absolutes that apply to them. Here are a few in my home:

a. You will go to church.
b. You will not watch certain movies.
c. You will be in at a certain time.
d. You will help with the chores.
e. You will show respect to others.

These are certainly not all of the possibilities. Finish the list for yourself. Parent, you have the right to enforce the absolutes. It is a part of training a child. Be a parent first and a friend second.

3. I still believe that you can raise godly children in an ungodly world.

I see examples of this all the time. I could go on and on about some students I know who are making a difference in their world. They are following God and preparing themselves to be used by Him. They have been raised and trained by godly parents and they *can, will,* and *are* excelling in life.

I have a good friend named Tim Van Douser. Tim and his wife, Stephanie, pastor a church in Millington, Tennessee. I have been honored to be a frequent ministry guest there throughout the years, and Dianna and I are blessed to call Tim and Stephanie our friends.

Tim and Stephanie have three boys who are all serving God. Recently I was having a phone conversation with Tim, and he was telling me a story about his youngest son, Jack. Jack, who feels called to be a missionary, had just gotten out of high school and was giving up his summer to go to Colombia to serve with our missionary friends Jack and Delores Simon. As Tim shared that with me, tears filled my eyes. Tim never knew it, but after we hung up, I prayed fervently for Jack.

I could share other stories, but suffice it to say, I still believe in this generation! I still believe good, godly students will make a difference in this world after I am gone. I still believe there will be a young man that I can pass my mantle to.

Though stories of rebellious students fill the news, we must never give up training our children. As parents or stepparents, we must lead with love as our compass. God will help us.

It was always humorous when students in my youth group or in youth camps where I spoke talked about leaving home. They were always so ready to leave. I would often hear this statement from students: "I cannot wait to leave home so that nobody can tell me what to do anymore." Well, guess what? Somebody will always be telling you what to do. You are going to grow up and get a job, and your employer will tell you what time to be at work, what to do while you are there, and when you can go home. People telling you what to do never ends. The best thing any of us can do is to learn to live within the authority structure of Scripture in all areas of our lives.

Paul put it like this to the church at Rome:

> Everyone must submit himself to the governing authorities, for there is no authority except that which God has established. The authorities that exist have been established by God. Consequently, he who rebels against the authority is rebelling against what God has instituted, and those who do so will bring judgment on themselves. For rulers hold no terror for those who do right, but for those who do wrong. Do you want to be free from fear from the one in authority? Then do what is right and he will commend you. For he is God's servant to do you good. But if you do wrong, be afraid, for he does not bear the sword for nothing. He is God's servant, an agent of wrath to bring punishment on the wrongdoer. Therefore, it is necessary to submit to the authorities, not only because of possible punishment but also because of conscience.
>
> —ROMANS 13:1–5

If an authority issue has you on the other side of courageous, work it out. First of all, work it out with God. Second, treat it as a heart issue and work it out with yourself. Third, work it out with the others who may be involved. God will honor that. Even if others do not receive your attempt, God will honor it. It will help you get back to courageous!

Questions for Discussion:

1. What are some dangers we face if there is no structure of authority in the home?
2. When you read God's Word, do you understand its clear authority structure? Discuss.
3. What are some ways we can build trust and respect in our lives as parents or leaders?
4. Are there wrong ways to exert your authority? Explain.
5. When authority is established, either rebellion or obedience will surface. How can we avoid rebellion in our kids, at our workplace, etc.?

THREE MEN
AND THEIR STORY

❧

*I*n this chapter, I am going to interview three
different men who all have stories to tell. They
have all been through a tragedy in their lives, but
they are all serving God today. Their stories will not
apply to everyone, but to those who are living where
these men have lived, I pray their stories will help
you through your pain.

First of all, I want to introduce a young man
named Jonathan. Jonathan is my youngest stepson.
His parents divorced when he was a small child, so
he has literally grown up without his mom and dad
living together under one roof. If your parents have
divorced and you are struggling, maybe Jonathan's
experience will help in some small way.

LYNN: How old were you when your parents
divorced?
JONATHAN: Seven.

LYNN: Do you remember your emotional response when you were told they were getting a divorce?
JONATHAN: Confusion. I remember coming home from school one day, and my mom was very upset. She was carrying around a bunch of papers and made me go into the other room. For some reason, that sticks in my mind.

LYNN: Does the pain of the divorce ever go away or at least lessen?
JONATHAN: No, it never goes away. I am not sure if it lessens or if you just get used to it. I think I just got used to it. It never went away, because at Christmas, for example, I always spent Christmas with either my mom or my dad, but never with both at the same time.

LYNN: What were your feelings when your mom remarried?
JONATHAN: I was initially opposed to it, but now it is a very, very good thing. The older I have gotten, the more I just want my mom to be happy. I don't want her to be alone in life, so I am happy about her getting remarried, for that and many other reasons. Same with my dad—I just want him to be happy.

LYNN: Do you remember what happened when your mom and I were dating, and we were all coming back from dinner one night? You and your brother were in the backseat of the car, and you leaned forward to inform me not to even

think about marrying your mother! Remember
that? *(smiling)*
JONATHAN: Yeah. *(laughter)*
LYNN: How old were you then?
JONATHAN: Ten. *(laughter)*

LYNN: What are some of the biggest challenges in
having a stepdad?
JONATHAN: At first, it was kind of strange seeing
my mom with someone else. The biggest challenge was getting used to someone else living in
our house with us. It seemed really strange until
I got used to that. It just takes time; everything in
that situation takes time. You cannot rush through
it.

LYNN: What advice would you give to other students whose parents have divorced?
JONATHAN: I would say these things:

1. Find someone you can talk to. I talked to
   a counselor at my school every week. Her
   name was Miss Walter, and she was very
   helpful to me. I really liked her. Talking
   helped me, and I think it would help others
   too.
2. Don't pick sides. You do not need to know
   all the details of why your parents split
   up. You love both of your parents equally.
   You don't need to be on anyone's side.
3. Don't criticize one parent to the other
   one. I think it is important not to bash

either parent to the other. I have tried not to do that, even when I am upset about something.

4. Talk to God a lot. He knows what you are going through, and He is the healer for the hurting. He is your answer in every situation.

LYNN: Thanks, man. Good stuff!
JONATHAN: Thanks! *(fist bump)*

The second man I want to introduce is Pastor Jason Whitehurst. Jason is the lead pastor of Music City Assembly of God in Nashville, Tennessee. I have been honored to be a ministry guest in his church several times. Jason and I have been friends for more than fifteen years. He and his wife, Tyra, have two beautiful children. They also have a tragic story that I cannot come close to relating to, but some of you can.

LYNN: Thank you for opening your heart to us. Tell us what happened with your son.

JASON: Let me start at the beginning. We had a son, Chase, who was born on December 22, 2002. He was born premature and weighed only one and a half pounds. The second he was born, the doctors whisked him away. We knew something was wrong. Almost two hours later, a nurse confirmed our fears with news that a doctor would soon be in to talk to us. When the doctor arrived, he told us Chase was not able to breathe on his own, and he did not offer much hope. They transferred us from one hospital to another, and the doctors there also gave us little hope that Chase would make it.

However, Chase hung in there. One day the doctor came in and told us that Chase had a rare heart condition and needed open-heart surgery. They felt that the surgery would correct the problem and that Chase would make a complete recovery. They were right, and three months after he was born, Chase went home from the hospital.

The next three months, Chase grew and developed normally. However, one day Tyra and I noticed him going into a blank stare and then breaking into laughter. That process repeated itself several times, and we knew something was wrong. When Chase was six months old, the doctor confirmed that he had both cerebral palsy and epilepsy.

Let me fast forward to April 24, 2006. I got up early that morning to go work out. Right before I walked out the door, Tyra called to me and asked if I could check on the kids before I left. I thought it was going to be a quick trip up the stairs and then out the door. However, when I opened the door to Chase's room, he was lying lifeless on the floor. I knew immediately that the life was gone from his body. I yelled for Tyra and began the process of trying to revive Chase. Nothing worked, and on April
ase went to heaven.

w you prayed many prayers for Chase's
ven prayed over him when I was there,

but he passed away anyway. As a lead pastor, that affected your faith, right?

JASON: Absolutely. I was angry and confused. I believed the Lord would have received more glory from healing Chase than from his death, and I did not understand.

LYNN: In people's attempts to comfort you, did the words they choose sometimes bring no comfort at all?

JASON: For sure. Several people came to me and said, "Well, Chase has received his ultimate healing now that he is in heaven." That did not help me at all. I wanted my son back.

LYNN: It has been a little over six years since Chase's death. How did you make it to this point?

JASON: Well, I went to a Christian counselor for a year. I literally poured out my heart. That helped so much.

LYNN: You had a daughter at that time, right?

JASON: Yes. Her name is McKenzie, and she was seven years old when Chase passed away. I want to tell you a quick story about how God used a seven-year-old to minister to Tyra and me. One day we were sitting around the house, feeling really sad about Chase. McKenzie got a couple of spiral note-books and gave them to my wife and me. She said she knew we were all sad about Chase right now, but just thought it would be good if we each had a note-book to write down good memories about him every time we felt sad. Several times God literally used a child to keep us going.

LYNN: So you were trying to survive emotionally while being there for your wife and daughter?
JASON: It was a battle spiritually, physically, and emotionally. I really questioned God.

LYNN: How did you get through that?
JASON: I was studying Psalms and discovered that David, the man after God's own heart, had also had some tough questions for God. I learned that my questions and my faith can coexist; I do not have to have it all figured out. I have not arrived, and I still struggle at times, but that really helped me.

LYNN: What would you say to someone struggling with the loss of a child right now?
JASON: So many people came to my house as soon as the word got out. A hearse, not an ambulance, came to get Chase. Several well-meaning people offered a lot of religious phrases, the same phrases I had used in my ministry as well. At that time, though, those phrases rang hollow.

I had a neighbor who was in his sixties. He and I have had a good relationship for a long time. He calls me "baby boy." As I handed Chase off to be taken away, my neighbor put his arms around me and said, "You are going to make it, baby boy. You are going to make it!" Something about those words helped me. Those are the words that have come back to me through the years. So those are my words to those struggling: *You are going to make it!* It will not ever be easy, but you are going to make it.

LYNN: Tell me about the orphanage you dedicated to Chase.
JASON: Tyra and I wanted Chase's legacy to continue, so we dedicated an orphanage in his name in Chiang Rai, Thailand. It is a boys' home that we are still supporting to this day.

LYNN: Thanks for opening your heart to us about Chase.
JASON: You're welcome.

I have an incredible amount of respect for Jason and Tyra. I cannot even imagine their pain. I also want you to know that on May 21, 2007, God blessed Jason and Tyra with another child, a daughter named Mia. Congratulations!

The third young man I want to introduce is Tavis England. Tavis was my oldest stepson in my first marriage. Tavis is now thirty-three years old and a father himself. Tavis and his wife, L. B., have three wonderful children. I am going to talk to Tavis about what it was like to grow up without a father. You see, his dad passed away in a car accident when Tavis was young.

LYNN: How old were you when your father passed away?
TAVIS: I was ten.

LYNN: Do you remember the day well?

TAVIS: Yes, I remember it like a movie I have seen a hundred times. We were living part-time on a college campus while my mom finished her degree. It was my first year to play organized football, and that night was going to be my first scrimmage. It was actually going to be the first time my dad was going to get to see me play. My brother and I already had our football stuff on when a trooper knocked on the door. He asked my brother Lucas and me to step outside. In just a couple of seconds, Mom started screaming from inside the apartment.

Then my Aunt Linda came running up the stairs, and she ran right by us, which was very unusual. The trooper left, and my aunt took my brother and me into bedroom and told us that our dad had been in an accident and did not make it. It didn't seem real. I cried, but mostly because everyone else was crying. I did not even realize the full extent of what was going on.

They drove us to the hospital, where I got to see my dad's body, but again, it just didn't seem real.

I do want to tell you about the night before the accident, though. My brother and I had gone to bed, but we were not going to sleep. We were cutting up, and finally Dad came into the room to calm us down. Before he left, he said, "Boys, I just want you to know that I really love you." We told him we knew it. Then he repeated it a couple more times. I didn't think anything about it then, but I do now. He also said, "Now, Tavis, you know that if anything happens to me, you are going to have to take care of your mom and brother." Looking back now, it seems like he almost knew something was going to happen.

LYNN: Did you get emotional at the funeral?
TAVIS: I was sitting by my Uncle Michael. I did not really cry until he started crying.

LYNN: Was there a time that remember when you did get really emotional about losing your dad?
TAVIS: Yes, when I was about to graduate from high school, I suddenly realized my dad was not going to be there. For whatever reason, that is the first time I remember just breaking down and crying hard about my dad. However, I have had those same breakdowns at other milestones in my life. When my kids were born, at college graduation, when I got married, etc. All of those milestones brought the same kind of breakdown in my life.

LYNN: Now that you are thirty-three, do you look back and see any lasting effects from growing up without your dad?
TAVIS: I feel really blessed to have had a great dad for ten years of my life. I think that I miss my dad more as an adult than I did as a kid. I just kind of grew up not knowing what I was missing, but now that I am grown, I miss him a lot. I miss his counsel and advice. There are times I just want to talk to him about a decision or get guidance about a situation, and I realize that my dad is not here.

I also am grieved by the fact that my dad will never meet my wife and children. My kids will grow up without ever knowing their grandfather. My grandfathers played such an important role in my growing-up years, and I regret that my children will not have that. On the other hand, growing up without a dad made me grow up faster and made me a lot tougher. I see those things as a positive. I just wish I had not had to lose my dad for that to happen.

LYNN: You are a dad now. How many kids do you have, and what are their ages?

TAVIS: I have a daughter who is six, a son who is four, and another son who is two months old.

LYNN: Did losing your dad as a child affect the way you parent your children?

TAVIS: It definitely makes me want to be a better parent. Being a good dad is important to me. My dad was a good dad, and I want to be a good dad. I feel that if I am not, then I will not be honoring his legacy. I put a lot of energy and effort into being a good parent. It is a high priority to me. I think it is because I realize that I might not be here tomorrow. I value every day I have with my kids. You never think about your parents dying until they do. Losing my dad at ten made me realize it can happen to anybody.

LYNN: What would you say to anyone who has lost a parent and may be struggling with that?

TAVIS: I can tell you this: God has been there for me! When you lose a parent, you feel like your safety net in life is gone, but it is not. It does feel like it, I agree, but God is and will always be your safety net. His love and ability outweigh that of any parent. He is always there for you. Trust Him to bring you through your loss. He has done that for me, and He will do it for you too!

I am proud of Tavis for many reasons, but mostly because he is serving the Lord and teaching his family the ways of God. I trust that his story will help someone who has suffered a similar loss.

I am thankful for all three of these men and their willingness to open their hearts. They know what it is to be on the other side of courageous, but God has brought (and is bringing) them back to courageous. He can do it for you too!

Questions for Discussion:

1. Can you relate to any of these stories? Which one, and why do you relate to it?
2. Have you dealt with the issues that have come your way as a result of your particular story in life?
3. Have you ever shared with anyone else an internal struggle of questioning God? If not, what is keeping you from doing that?
4. Has your experience brought anything positive to your life? If so, what is it?
5. Have you been able to use your experience to help someone else? If so, how?

BLENDED FAMILY

*I*n 1973, Steve Kuhnau founded Smoothie King in Louisiana. A smoothie is a thick drink that contains fruit blended with milk, juice, or yogurt. Kuhnau had been experimenting with smoothie recipes for years, adding ingredients such as yogurt, protein powder, and vitamins to his concoctions. Over the next three decades, Smoothie Kings began popping up all over the country and made the term *smoothie* a household word. Now you can get smoothies in restaurants and even bottled at the store.

Though Kuhnau is the most notable founder of a business featuring this type of drink, the smoothie itself actually dates back much farther. Kristine Miles wrote an article for Green Smoothie Community called "The History of Blending." In that article, she talks about the Indian lassi, a creamy blend of yogurt, fruits, and spices. This drink originated around 1000 BC and could well have been the world's first smoothie.(3)

My first experience with anything close to a smoothie was a drink called an Orange Julius. When

I was a teenager, Orange Julius stores came to the mall in Oklahoma City. Every time I would go to the mall, I would get one. It was orange juice blended with milk, sugar, and vanilla. It was awesome!

I have tasted many smoothies in my travels. They have some kind of smoothie store in almost every town I visit. I have experimented with several types of blends, some of which I love and others that I don't. When you start blending things together, sometimes the result is sweet, but sometimes it is bitter.

My wife and I are avid coffee drinkers. I love a bold coffee and am a frequent visitor to Starbucks. My wife loves flavored coffees, her favorite being French vanilla. She will go to Starbucks with me, but she usually gets one of their blended drinks. At home, it is Dunkin' Donuts French vanilla for us. It's not my favorite, but it's hers — guys, you know where I am going with that! Enough said.

Anyway, since I spend a lot of time on the road, I only drink the French vanilla when I am home. If I hit a stretch when I am home for several days, I am soon very ready for a good, plain cup of coffee. I'm just not much for a lot of blended flavors, especially in my coffee.

On the other hand, my dad is from the generation where he just wants a good old cup of Folgers. He thinks it is ridiculous that I pay what I do for a cup of coffee. Every time I am in Oklahoma City, I try to have breakfast with my dad. We have the "coffee" discussion almost every time. When he visits in our home, Dianna will concede her French vanilla for a couple of days. He is one who cannot even fake his way through a cup of coffee blended with any other flavor.

That being said, there is a huge difference between blending ingredients, fruits, and vitamins and blending different kinds of people. There is no comparison. Each of us brings a certain personality and belief system with us. While there are times when we must give direction to both, we never want to take away anyone's uniqueness or identity. Therefore, blending people together is a far greater challenge than making a smoothie.

There are many different statistics regarding the divorce rate in our nation, but I think I am safe in saying it hovers right around the 50 percent mark. At least, that is what most of the stats I have seen say. As the divorce rate continues to escalate, more and more children are growing up in broken homes. When one of their parents decides to remarry, that creates what has come to be known as a *blended family*. This creates new challenges in and of itself, but if the new spouse also has children, well, there are even more challenges to face. The more people involved, the greater the challenge.

In the January 6, 2010 edition of *Psychology Today*, Sean Cort wrote an article called "Helpful Advice for Blended Families." In that article, he points out that "when you remarry into a family with children or you take your children into a new family, the choices you make and the perspective you live will have even more of a compound effect." I can confirm this from my own personal experience.

In a blended family, at first everyone is carefully watching everyone else. But in the process of getting to know the other members of the family, you also have to live with them. Here are some things I have learned about the process:

1. KEEP GOD AT THE FOREFRONT OF EVERYTHING IN YOUR HOME.

   a. Attend church together.
   b. Discuss the Bible and the things of God.
   c. Do devotions together, and don't forget communion.
   d. Live the life of a believer in your home as well as in public.
   e. Trust God in every situation.

2. RECOGNIZE THAT EVERYONE IS VALUABLE.

   a. No person is better or more important than another.
   b. Everyone's opinion will be heard. It may not be carried through on, but it will be heard.
   c. Personal attacks on others' opinions or name calling is not acceptable—ever!

3. ESTABLISH BOUNDARIES AND RULES.

   a. If boundaries and rules are not established and verbalized, they will never be carried out or abided by.

    b. Adjust your rules when needed. As kids get older, things need to be adjusted. Do not treat a sixteen-year-old like an eight-year-old.

    c. Inform everyone of the consequences if rules are broken. Carry that out. Just saying it is not enough.

4. KEEP PRIORITIES IN LINE.

    a. Relational priorities are vital, and your most important relationship, except with God, is your relationship with your spouse. Work on it, and give it priority. Have a date night with just the two of you every week, if possible.

    b. Family fun is a must. Do something fun as a family every week. I know this gets harder as kids get older, but make the effort to get together and laugh. It creates great memories.

    c. There is value in time spent together. Sometimes it does not matter what you do as much as the fact that you are spending time together.

5. TAKE IT SLOW AND BE PATIENT.

    a. Bonding with your new spouse's children will not happen overnight. Take it slowly, and do not give up.

b. Never make it seem as though your new spouse has to choose between you or their children. They may have to choose between the opinions of each at times, but not the people. Do not take it personally if they agree with their children. I know I have been wrong at least once in my life!

c. It is worth the wait. Again, I speak from experience. Being a blended family can work with the help of the Lord. Everyone working together for the good of the family brings great rewards.

It has been said many ways at many times, but it is true: children are the ones who are hurt the most in divorce. They are the innocent victims. If you are going into a blended-family situation, consider the children.

I read a great article on Helpguide.org that had been updated in May 2012. It was written by Gina Kemp, M.A.; Jeanne Segal, Ph.D.; and Lawrence Robinson. In the updated article they included a new section dedicated to children on "bonding with your new blended family." Focusing on the children, they reminded us that children need to feel the following:

a. Safe and secure: Children want to be able to count on parents and stepparents. Children of divorce have already felt the upset of having people they trust let them down, and they may not be eager to give a second chance to a new stepparent.

b. Loved: Kids like to see and feel your affection, although it should be a gradual process

c. Seen and valued: Kids often feel invisible and unimportant when it comes to decision making in the new blended family. Recognize their role in the family when you make decisions.

d. Heard and emotionally connected: Creating an honest and open environment free of judgment will help kids feel heard and emotionally connected to a new stepparent. Show them that you can view the situation from their perspective.

e. Appreciated and encouraged: Children of all ages respond to praise and encouragement and like to feel appreciated for their contributions.

f. Limits and boundaries: Children may not think they need limits, but a lack of boundaries sends a signal that the child is unworthy of the parent's time, care, and attention. As a new stepparent, you shouldn't immediately step in as the enforcer, but you should work with your spouse to set limits.

That is great stuff! I hope you find it helpful.

Any family structure will have challenges and its fair share of ups and downs. I have made so many mistakes in this area, yet things are still intact in my home. I am grateful to God for my wife, Dianna. She is the rock of our home. Her gentle nature is something I long for in my own life. She has taught me so much, and I love her for it.

Right before Dianna and I were married, I sat her boys down and had a talk with them. I told them that I was not going to try and be their dad. They already had a dad, and I was not here to replace him. I also informed them in that same talk that there are two things I will not accept from them:

1. They will not disrespect their mother. If they do, I will call them on it.
2. They will not tear up the house. Since I am the one paying for the house, they will be in trouble if they damage it.

We have had limited issues with both. When we do, I always remind them that I set these boundaries from the beginning.

I was on the other side of courageous because of a broken family. In my brokenness, God honored me with a great new family. I am blessed! I am going to conclude this chapter by giving you several verses that will help you in all situations, especially in your family:

"Each of you should look not only to your own interests, but also to the interests of others" (Phil. 2:4).

"Bear with each other and forgive whatever grievances you may have against one another. Forgive as the Lord forgave you" (Col. 3:13).

"If it is possible, as far as it depends on you, live at peace with everyone" (Rom. 12:18).

"May the God who gives endurance and encouragement give you a spirit of unity among yourselves as you follow Christ Jesus" (Rom. 15:5).

"Above all, love each other deeply, because love covers over a multitude of sins" (1 Pet. 4:8).

"Grace and peace be yours in abundance" (1 Pet. 1:2).

Questions for Discussion:

1. Why is it so important to keep God first in all family situations?
2. Is every person in your home valued equally? Why or why not?
3. Discuss the value of rules and boundaries for our kids. Are they still important today?
4. What are some challenges you face in keeping your priorities in line concerning your relationships?
5. What are some action steps you can take to make your family unit healthier in every way?

DEDICATION

*T*o all my friends and family members who stopped to pour in the healing oil when I was beaten and bloody from the cares of life. Thank you for being a Good Samaritan to me. I will never forget it as long as I live.

Notes

1 — "Why Great Men Fall", Wayde Goodall, New Leaf Press (pg. 114)
2 — "Strengthening Your Grip", Charles Swindoll, Word Books (pgs. 99-100)
3 — "Green Smoothie Community" (History of Blending) March 15, 2012

About the Author

$\mathcal{F}$ or almost 30 years Lynn Wheeler has been traveling and proclaiming the truth of Gods Word. Lynn travels both nationally and internationally ministering in a variety of ways, including Men's Conferences, Missions Emphasis services, conventions and Spiritual Emphasis Weeks.

Since the year 2000, this ministry has been following the mandate from God to help provide inspiration, instruction, and financing to raise up and establish new churches in the country of Ukraine.

A dynamic author, Lynn has written two other books, "Living Free" and "The F.O.G. is Rolling In." He has also been a contributing author to five other Christian books.

Lynn and his wife, Dianna, currently live in Arkansas and have three wonderful children.

INFORMATION

*T*o schedule Lynn for services or for more information about his ministry:

Lynn Wheeler Ministries
PO Box 1160
Greenbrier, AR. 72058
(501) 679-6566 (office)

LW7460@aol.com
www.lynnwheelerministries.com

Acknowledgements

*T*hank you to my faithful friend, ministry partner and wife, Dianna. You are a God send! Thank you for standing with me. I love you.

Thank you to the Board of Directors of Lynn Wheeler Ministries:

Herbert Cooper, Lead Pastor, Peoples Church in Oklahoma City, Okla.
Fred Franks, Lead Pastor, Christian Life in Orange Beach, AL.
Gary Nelson, Businessman, Oklahoma City, Okla.

Their counsel, guidance and friendship is so vital to me and my ministry. I appreciate you guys. Thanks for all you do to help me succeed.

CPSIA information can be obtained at www.ICGtesting.com
Printed in the USA
LVOW120349291112

309298LV00001B/1/P